au·then·tic

au·then·tic

RELENTLESSLY PURSUING JESUS

KYLE HOWELL

I dedicate this book to my best friend and amazing wife who was a huge support through this whole process. Also, I want to thank my Authentic Church family where I have learned about how church is supposed to be done.

Contents

Chapter 1
Why Authentic?

It's so uncomfortable when something tries to hold you back, from telling the truth. But in the end, when some things need to be heard, then it's the time to say what's real.

-Unknown

I live in South Texas and I see a lot of Mexican restaurants. A lot of these restaurants will say they are "authentic" Mexican restaurants. Sometimes I wonder how different they really are from one another. I'm not a food connoisseur, so I'm not sure I would be the one to put these places to the test. I don't even have a sense of smell (that's another story). So whether a place says it has authentic

1

Mexican food, it doesn't really faze me. I just want to know it's clean and has awesome tortillas.

Some people don't take this into consideration. "I grew up on the real stuff. Don't give me any of that fake junk posing as the real thing." So sometimes whether you value authenticity comes down to what you've had before, where you're from, and whether you have strong taste buds. Right? In other areas of life, authenticity is less subjective and more a matter of truth.

When I was younger, I collected baseball cards. I remember hearing stories about people finding old Babe Ruth or Honus Wagner cards in their attics and selling them for small fortunes. I am now about thirty years removed from when I collected those and am sad to learn that my best cards might be able to get me five or ten dollars. So I guess I'll hide them in the attic and maybe my great, great, great grandkid will find them and get a few hundred dollars. For the most part, the worth of a baseball card does not depend on subjective opinion. No one cares about its sentimental value to you or your family. A baseball card is either the real thing with real value, or not. The same is true for jewelry, paintings, and autographs.

So why am I choosing to talk about authenticity? Because the church could use a heavy dose of it. It seems as if those of us in the church have been trying to remove some of its authentic teachings and beliefs so we can reach more people and draw them in. The irony is the people we are trying to reach are turned away from the church too often because it lacks authenticity.

I realize there are plenty of books out there from guys like me trashing the church and saying we're all stupid and need to change. I don't mean to do that. I just want to point out what I have been seeing in our culture. People unequivocally want to see transparency, openness, and an authentic faith. So how do we approach authenticity in the church, like Mexican food or baseball cards? If we take the Mexican-food approach, we're going to end up right where most people find themselves in America. "This is what I think it should be." "I've grown up with this flavor of church." "I'm not much of a church person, so it has to be only a special occasion, or I go to please someone else."

I like the word *authentic* because it seems to echo what we're missing. It is also a word I hear repeatedly from those outside the church or those who have been hurt by the church. This is what they're craving from the church. It shouldn't be a burden. It's an enormous opportunity for the church—God's people—to examine what it is we are doing and what it is we should do.

My hope in writing this book is to push the church to hear this cry from people and to get a sense of urgency not to live for ourselves or make the church some kind of therapeutic moral group, but to take on a literal and authentic approach to living the way the Bible calls us.

I want to show how to live a life of reckless abandon for God, how to live out the Gospel the way the early church did, and see if it's possible to re-create that life in our day and time. Many today are repulsed by the church. Others are simply not interested in it. Part of the reason is because we as the church are not correctly and clearly living differently from the world. We either live completely separated from the world, or we live exactly like it with no difference. Rarely do we correctly balance being noticeably different with a worldview bent toward God, yet still being right in the middle of the mess, hurt, and confusion of this world.

Jesus prayed in John 17 that His followers would be protected from the enemy, not that they would be taken out of the world. Jesus was saying they had a mission and He was sending them out to do His work. That's the church. This is where we commonly get the phrase "in the world, but not of the world." That's what I know God has done: He has strategically placed His people—the church—in the darkness so we can shine His light for people to find Him.

I want to examine what the Bible says about being a follower of Christ. We're going to look at the early church and see what they actually did and how that translates into what we're supposed to do today. We have such heated debates in the church worldwide about what it means to be a follower of Christ: how it looks, how we're supposed to look, and even how the church is supposed to look. Why don't we just take the Bible for what it says? That's what I'm attempting to do through this book.

I have to admit, I don't know how this is going to affect me. Even though I'm trying to follow this approach, I have never laid it all out and examined it this closely. So I fully expect to do a lot of growing myself.

4

Finally, I hope to challenge those of you who have so many issues with the church that you feel as if you no longer need to go. I understand you may have some major frustrations with your experiences in church, but don't give up on it altogether (see Hebrews 10:24-25). And don't go out of your way to blow up about your church experiences on social media.

A perfect example of the church being the church was when Priscilla and Aquila first met Apollos. They saw he was educated, knew the scriptures, and had a great speaking ability, but he didn't have the whole truth about the Gospel. They didn't yell out in the meeting, "Heretic!" Instead they invited him to their house after the meeting and explained the truth to him more clearly. As a result he became more effective and God used him greatly.

For those of you who have never been in church, or feel it has nothing for you, I want you to examine what it is really about. If you're going to reject something as huge as what Jesus and His followers claim about Him, at least hear the whole message. If there is absolutely no way any of the claims happened, then you can go on with your life and have nothing to do with God or the church again.

Something monumental needs to happen in the church. Something big needs to change. What I read in the New Testament is not what I see in Christianity and the church today. I know I am not alone in that conviction. Haven't you ever noticed that anytime anyone commits repeated crimes of sexual or physical harassment, most of the time the ones who were attacked stay silent until one person speaks up? Then they feel empowered, or safe, to come out in the open.

That's the same type of movement I see in the church today. Some people are examining the Scriptures and are coming to the right conclusion that something is wrong and someone needs to stand up and be the voice. Doing so inevitably causes others to express the same convictions. Once one person crosses that threshold, others can cross through that doorway as well.

I am asking you to take a serious look at the church today. Examine what you are doing in it and what is happening where you are. And then consider crossing the threshold into an authentic, genuine, and real walk into the unknown, but exciting life with Christ that I believe we were created for, but missed somewhere along the way.

Chapter 2

Did They Have Something That I don't?

"For when I am weak, then I am strong."
– Paul

Are you familiar with the phrase "the elephant in the room"? It means there's a big issue that everyone knows about and is probably thinking about, but no one will say anything about it.

There is a large number of people in the church whose elephant in the room is: "Did the apostles and early church have something that I don't?" A lot of us tend to read the Bible and hear about what happened in the early church and assume they must have had, I don't know, an extra faith gene, or

7

something. Maybe they were given more power and ability to do certain things that we just can't do. Every month a new superhero movie comes out, so I think we start to equate the first-church heroes with superhuman beings. Right?

If this is left unexamined, it can become a major obstacle to us taking steps in faith and doing more, or being used by God in a much more powerful way. Maybe I'm just making some overly dramatic claims. On the other hand, pastors can be pretty dramatic to bring effect and punch to their sermons. Am I just doing that to sell a book? Having been a pastor for many years now, in different places, and in different titles, I have witnessed this from people.

I remember when I wasn't a Christian, and even when I was a brand-new Christian, I had a feeling of inadequacy and inferiority. It wasn't because everyone I knew in the church was condescending to me. It was almost like a Matrix feeling. You remember that movie? When a friend and I went to see it while we were in college, we came back to our apartment and he said, "Dude, what if the Matrix is true? What if this isn't real now?" So we both decided our professors and administrators at school were just trying to keep the truth from us. So we stopped doing school work. Just kidding!

Do you ever feel that way? Do you feel as if everyone in church around you just "gets it" more than you do? Do you feel as if they have this extra gene that predisposes them to living a Christian life better than you do? You're not alone. I've come to see there are a lot of people who feel this way. I don't think it's limited to people who don't go to church; people inside the church have these same misconceptions.

My story of coming to Christ started when I went to a Christian college to play baseball. I wasn't there for the Bible classes. I was just there to get some basics out of the way, play some ball, and party. God had a different plan, however. In the first semester of college, I gave my life to Christ. That summer I had a feeling and just believed God wanted me to be in ministry (even though I had no clue where, or even what that meant).

So I started taking Bible classes. I remember feeling as if I was the stupidest person in the world when it came to the Bible. Many in those classes knew the Bible pretty well because they had grown up under their dads who were pastors, or had come from families that were committed Christ followers. So I was constantly saying stupid things (even when I thought they were true) and feeling as if there was no way I was going to get what the Bible was talking about.

One time the professor asked us to name the ten plagues in Egypt during the Old Testament. I was sure I remembered one, so I said it. "Killer bees," I said confidently. Nope. But I made everyone laugh. If you're not laughing now, then you must be like I was then. So there was no way I thought I could be used by God, let alone be a pastor.

So look, I get it. I know people who never pick up the Bible to read it consistently for the same reason. It's hard to get and these folks feel as if there was a pre-message or introductory class to being a Christian that others secretly took, but no one's telling anyone about it. With that in mind, I'm speaking to those of you who may be reading this right now and feel as if the early church, the apostles, and those we read about in the Bible were just a different breed of people. They were unlike us, so that's why God could do His will and works through them. Right?

I have a verse for those of you who think that way:

Elijah was a human being, even as we are. He prayed earnestly that it would not rain, and it did not rain on the land for three and a half years. Again he prayed, and the heavens gave rain, and the earth produced its crops.

-James 5:17

So James is telling us about the power of prayer and prayer from a righteous person and he brings up Elijah. This is a big-time guy, the greatest prophet, from the Old Testament. God did some mind-blowing things through this guy. One time Elijah went to King Ahab. He was an evil King, married to the infamous Jezebel. Yeah that one! Even if you don't know the Bible very well, you've probably been called a Jezebel, or maybe you called your mother-in-law a Jezebel. Don't do that! What about Bobby Bouche? You remember his mom calling his girlfriend that? I digress.

So Elijah goes to the King and tells him, based on God's plan, that there will be no rain on the land for three and a half years. Now here's the really bold part: Jezebel and many of the people worshipped a false god named Baal. This god was known to be the god of rain and bountiful harvests. So Elijah's like, "Listen here: the rain's gonna stop for a few years until I speak it back."

Now he wasn't doing this and taking the credit. They knew he was a prophet of God. So he speaks this to the King, it happens, and Elijah goes in to hiding. And then he is fed by ravens. Just a typical Tuesday, right? No! I mean this is just crazy. This is some wild, mountain man, Discovery Channel type stuff. So God takes cares of him.

Then Elijah faces off with some false prophets of the King. Not just a few, but 850 to be exact (450 for Baal and 400 for Asherah). Read it; it's insane! He basically says, "Ok, you guys build an altar, call out to your god, and I'll do the same. Whosever god shows up will be the true God."

So they try for hours and hours, yelling, cutting themselves, and nothing happens. Elijah even taunts them. Then he prays, God shows up, brings down fire, and completely consumes the offering and altar. What an amazing thing to witness, especially after all the time the huge group of false prophets had spent trying to summon their gods, and yet not so much as a car backfired. The people were shocked.

And just to end the account of this prophet Elijah, do you know how he exited the world? This is the way to make an exit. I want to exit the world the way he did. I won't hold my breath, though. God took him on a chariot of fire with horses and a whirlwind. Elijah has left the building...on a chariot of fire!

I want to preach the most amazing sermon, then one million people get saved, then I solve the world's hunger problem, and finally I punch Satan in the face and he falls down and out cold, then God takes me up. Right? I'll probably die on the toilet, though.

Anyway, this is the same Elijah that we're told is just like we are, in that he was just a human being. He didn't have an extra faith gene. He wasn't born with some kind of heavenly frequency that caused him to tap into heaven. And he didn't have God's unlisted cell phone number. He was just a regular guy. Let's normalize him for a second.

So what was it then that made a difference? I believe that's a great question to ask and to speculate an answer for. It was not his amazing innate abilities, but his faithfulness to God. To be used by God we have to be faithful and obedient to Him, right in the middle of where He wants us.

When I read about these guys and God doing big-time things through them, they were not sitting comfortably in their cozy churches, living for themselves, with no connection with the outside world. No, they were out in the jungle, so to speak, of the world, being a light in the dark place. Right? Don't you read that too?

I've examined my life honestly and, in church and my own prayer times, have prayed for God to do some enormous, God-shaking things. That's not bad. We should want to see God show up and do His thing on a grand scale. I want to see some mountain-moving types of things. Am I alone in that? But what I've come to realize is when God was doing these things, He always did it when the people were in His will and in the middle of some struggle, or faith-testing moment. They were in the middle of the jungle of the broken world. They weren't playing it safe.

When I look at so many of the times when I prayed those prayers, however, I am almost exclusively in a safe place with little to no faith needed. You know what I mean? I may be sitting in church, with a group of good people, having a good time, and asking God to shoot a lightning bolt down the middle of the room (supernaturally not breaking the roof or floor, so we don't have to pay for it), just so we can know He heard us. Right? That may not be our exact prayer, or yours, but I bet it's not too far off.

Instead, I believe He's calling for us to step out in faith and be right in the middle of the messiness that is our world, where we have to rely on faith and then shoot those genuine, from-the-heart, faithful prayers to God and see what He does. I'm not saying He has to do anything, or that this is some type of fool-proof formula for coercing Him to move. I just believe that is the type of faith, boldness, and willingness He is calling for and looking for in His followers.

What about the disciples in the early church? Remember when Peter and John had an encounter with the Sanhedrin, who threatened them and told them to stop preaching about Jesus? Look at what their response was when they reported back to the other believers:

On their release, Peter and John went back to their own people and reported all that the chief priests and the elders had said to them. When they heard this, they raised their voices together in prayer to God. "Sovereign Lord," they said, "you made the heavens and the earth and the sea, and everything in them. You spoke by the Holy Spirit through the mouth of your servant, our father David:

"'Why do the nations rage and the peoples plot in vain? The kings of the earth rise up and the rulers band together against the Lord and against his anointed one.'

Indeed Herod and Pontius Pilate met together with the Gentiles and the people of Israel in this city to conspire against your holy servant Jesus, whom you anointed. They did what your power and will had decided beforehand should happen. Now, Lord, consider their threats and enable your servants to speak your word with great boldness. Stretch out your hand to heal and perform signs and wonders through the name of your holy servant Jesus."

After they prayed, the place where they were meeting was shaken. And they were all filled

with the Holy Spirit and spoke the word of God
boldly.

-Acts 4:23-31

I absolutely love to read those passages! I get equally
excited and convicted. I get excited because it's awesome to
see the believers put their faith in action even when they had no
clue what would happen next. Their lives were at stake. This
is a big-time, Braveheart moment here: "They may take our
lives, but they'll never take our faaaaaaith!" So I'm hugely
encouraged and pumped about their willingness to follow God,
even in the most unpredictable, scary moments of their lives
(up to that point). Simply by placing their faith in God and
having an unwavering commitment to His mission to get His
word proclaimed to everyone, God showed up.

These are the types of verses that push me and give me
goosebumps. But these verses are equally convicting because
it's a whole lot easier to read this, thank them for their
commitment, and talk with others about how cool this event
was than it is to model their faithfulness.

So it comes down to our obedience and faithfulness to
God. Right? That may seem simple, but I think it's true. It's
fun to talk about God doing big things. It's popular to say we
want to be sold out to Him and nothing else. But our actions
don't follow.

I'm reminded of a sitcom where the main character was
informed that it would be a good idea for him to declare

bankruptcy. He didn't understand how the process worked, though. So he dramatically walked out of his office to where the other workers were and said in a powerful and liberating way, "I declare bankruptcy!" Another coworker let him know that was not how it worked.

That's how far too many Christians are from living a Christian life. It's not enough to say "I believe Jesus is the only way to salvation. I believe people need to hear about Jesus. I believe in the mission that Jesus left the church to do" and have a mental assent to those statements. The Christian is called to be active in fulfilling them in their daily walks. Empty words that are not backed up by actions are pointless. "Faith without works is dead" (James 2:26), right?

Let me ask you a question that I sometimes ask the people of our church: Why do you go to church? I could probably get some lengthy explanations. "Someone made me." "We've always done it." "It just feels right." "I think I'm supposed to." "I like the music." "I like to listen to you, Kyle, because your voice is angelic and you speak amazing truths." Something like that maybe - ha!

If you come simply for affirmation that what you are doing is ok, or if you come with no expectation of being challenged, you're missing so much. I want you to be encouraged, lifted up, and helped through life. I really do. Whenever I preach, teach, or talk to someone, I don't build what I say around the idea that I want to make that person feel the pain and leave belittled and worse off than when he or she came in. I don't.

But listen: we need to be challenged. We need to be confronted sometimes and shown the truth. We need to constantly assess our lives to see if we are following God the way He wants. Look, even as I am writing this, looking at it, and hearing it out loud, it just doesn't sound spiritual. It might even sound a little legalistic. But hear me out on this: it's not legalistic to examine our lives and compare what we find to the way God shows us in Scripture. Paul said this:

> Examine yourselves to see whether you are in the faith; test yourselves. Do you not realize that Christ Jesus is in you—unless, of course, you fail the test?

> -2 Corinthians 13:5

So the obvious question is: "What is this test and how do I tell whether I am in the faith?" Anytime we hear "test" we get nervous, or anxious, or we want to run the other way. But if, for example, you're checking out a new axe, how do you test it to see whether it's a good axe? Do you admire how shiny it is? Do you read up on what kind of wood the handle is made of? Do you go online and read about iron and who the first person was to use an axe? That's crazy talk. You swing that axe on a tree and see how good and sharp it is. Without actually using it, you're just like me watching baseball games and perfecting my swing in the air. "Oooo. That is a pretty swing." Or when I pretend to throw or catch a football while

I'm watching a game. Still trying to live the dream. Maybe I'll get the call?

It's the same principle in the Christian walk. If all we do is show up to church and listen to the pastor and then sit around and talk about what God says to us in the Bible about how He wants us to live and act in this world, then we are failing at living the life He wants us to. I know those are strong words, but I don't want you to be inactive and just soaking in information. We have to be doers of the word.

So, with that in mind, how did God use people in the first church in such powerful and impactful ways? How was David able to take down a seemingly undefeatable warrior? How was Paul able to have this unshakable faith wherever he went when his life was always on the line? First, because they served the one and only all-powerful God of creation, and second, because they were willing to step out in faith to where God had called them.

I've come to learn that getting to this point where God does some blow-your-mind, amazing, world-changing stuff requires us to first be faithful in the small stuff. That's where He trains and prepares us.

Chapter 3
Life Together

Enjoy life. There's plenty of time to be dead.
— *Hans Christian Andersen*

There are a lot of family experiences and standards of living I just can't relate to. I cannot sit down with someone from the royal family over a spot of tea and discuss the struggles of life the same way they can. While they have struggles just like I do, our stories are going to be decidedly different. "Kyle, can you believe I once had to share my private jet with my cousin, the Duke of Earl?" I can't even relate enough to speak of a funny, unreal, but possible story they might understand.

I bring this up because there are times when I read about the early church in the book of Acts and see it as a completely foreign concept. Are you with me on that? Maybe a small percentage of you have experienced this, but the vast majority of Christianity hasn't. I'm not trying to create some rift in people's perception of the church, but I cannot relate to the way the church in Acts was. So let's talk about what they did and how their culture perceived it. We as the church today need to talk about this, wrestle with it, and see how it should look today.

I love to read Acts and see what God was doing:

> They devoted themselves to the apostles' teaching and to fellowship, to the breaking of bread and to prayer. Everyone was filled with awe at the many wonders and signs performed by the apostles. All the believers were together and had everything in common. They sold property and possessions to give to anyone who had need. Every day they continued to meet together in the temple courts. They broke bread in their homes and ate together with glad and sincere hearts, praising God and enjoying the favor of all the people. And the Lord added to their number daily those who were being saved.

> - Acts 2:42-47

I know you can't just completely model your church after these few simple verses, because there is more to a church than that. I am convinced, however, that this is the core and the bones of what church should be about. I've been in church for many years and have seen many different models of how church is done. I've been part of churches of different sizes, some of which had only a few programs and others that were program-driven. Many of the programs and ministries we do in church are not bad, but they can become distracting.

I've read many books on church leadership and one of the stats that appears consistently is the 20/80 principle: 20 percent of the people in a church do 80 percent of the work. I have seen this principle played out exactly as those numbers claim. If we're not careful, we can overuse people and burn them out without even hitting on two of the biggest callings of the church—reaching people and making disciples. It doesn't mean churches can't have gyms and athletic complexes. We just can't let them draw our attention away from the most important calling.

So back to those verses. What are the core things—the bones of the church? These are the things I would argue have to be front and center:

Scripture

Are we basing everything we do on the word of God? Just in my conversations with people in the churches I have been part of, most churched people say they don't read their Bibles. Because they don't read their Bibles, they are unfamiliar with many of the most common stories. We're living in a time where people are not able to make a noticeable distinction between Superman and Jesus. Far too many would not even be able to confidently tell you whether the Nativity or the latest fantasy/action movie might be a story from the Bible.

If you're not shaking your head, then you might fall into this group. Ha! That's ok. When I first went to college, I was not a Christian. When I started taking Bible classes, some of my answers fit into these categories. "Are you serious, Kyle?" "What? No...c'mon. Who would think that? Haha! Ha ha."

The first thing that was essential to the early church was Scripture. We must read it and make it an essential part of our lives. It's not rocket science (unless you buy a really difficult translation and have never read the Bible before). If we don't read it and get ourselves familiar with it, then we will never know what it says and thus be ignorant to how we are supposed to live and function through this life as followers of Christ.

Look at how the apostles and the early church responded to God's word—they were devoted to it. It doesn't say they had a pretty good appreciation for it, or they read it frequently, or they had a copy of it sitting on a table for everyone who came into their house to see. They devoted themselves to it. If you're devoted to something, your life is going to be altered by it and what it says.

Think about these two things: my marriage and college football. One of these should be more important to me. Maybe there are guys out there who just need to hear this one message. Both of them could be important to me. Now if I say they are equally important to me, then there is going to be a problem. I will either have a counselor in my future, an angry wife, or most likely both.

College football is fun to watch. I have my favorite team and I will usually watch every one of their games. But (and here's where I hopefully get points with my wife) my devotion does not lie with college football. My devotion is to my marriage and keeping it strong and God-honoring. College football is just something fun to watch. I'm not devoted to it. I don't even personally know any of the players or the coaches. So devotion should be more than a mere appreciation for something. It moves you to action.

Fellowship

After scripture, the early church was devoted to fellowship. Typically when I think of fellowship, I think about a big potluck meal prepared by people in the church. I'm from Oklahoma and have done a ton of ministry in Texas, so I'm familiar with these meals. It's like going to Golden Corral, but with paper plates and plastic wrap. Right? I still think they are really good, though. And I think they accomplish part of what God wants His people to do—enjoy being around each other and Him.

God doesn't just want us to sit around each other with the Bible opened and singing songs for one hour a week. The picture of us being part of the church is for us to do life together. Our depiction of that is far too small, however. Too often church is seen as a building that we go to once a week (or, if you're super spiritual, maybe two days a week).

I want to stretch your mind by saying God calls us to form strong bonds with people. We should know what is going on with people we worship with. One of the best illustrations of this concept in Scripture is the church being compared to a human body:

> Just as a body, though one, has many parts, but all its many parts form one body, so it is with Christ.

> -1 Corinthians 12:12

He is referring to the church that is in Christ. He continues in verse 26 with, "If one part suffers, every part suffers with it; if one part is honored, every part rejoices with it." I like this illustration because I can understand it. It's not too complicated. Maybe it was for people like me.

I jumped off a porch one time going toward my truck, put my foot in a hole, and sprained my ankle pretty good. We lived right off Main Street in a fairly big town, so a few cars drove by as this train wreck was happening. It was embarrassing as I was going down, arms flailing about like I was swimming in the air. But even worse, it hurt. The pain my ankle was having was shared with the rest of my body, only my left ankle was not laughing at the hurt right ankle. "Haha!

You're an idiot, righty! Klutz!" No, all of me shared in the pain.

I banged my head on a towel rack, getting in the shower one time. I literally saw stars! I didn't even know that was possible outside of cartoons. I was worried my wife would find me in there. That would've been embarrassing, almost as embarrassing as writing about it in this book.

So, like I said, I get it. It makes sense to speak about how the church should function by comparing it to a fully functioning body. But that's not what we typically see being personified. Usually we see a bunch of separate pieces occasionally gathering around each other, more out of tolerance than out of love and enjoyment. The connection to one another is lacking. But the early church had this real fellowship and enjoyment around each other the way a family would. It was different.

Acts 2:44-45 shows us this beautiful, but unusual picture of how this played out:

> All the believers were together and had everything in common. They sold property and possessions to give to anyone who had need.
>
> -Acts 2:44-45

It was real devotion, because it drove them to action and to be different.

The breaking of bread

The breaking of bread had two meanings: eating meals together and celebrating the Lord's Supper or Communion. Let me talk about the eating meals together first. This is a carry-over from fellowship. That's where I briefly mentioned the eating part. Verse 46 says, "They broke bread in their homes and ate together with glad and sincere hearts." Again I want this to challenge your perception of what it means to be in the body of Christ—the church. Look at this scripture and see what it's telling us. Church is not supposed to be a social club where we come in and meet some people we really don't know but can help us out from time to time. Those are acquaintances. The Bible, on the other hand, paints our relationships as if we should be family.

Then there is the Lord's Supper. I'm only going to make mention of this, not refer to it constantly. I'm not downplaying it; I'm just not going to spend much time on it. Paul, quoting Jesus, was clear on when and how to do this:

This is my body, which is for you; do this in remembrance of me." In the same way, after supper he took the cup, saying, "This cup is the new covenant in my blood; do this, whenever you drink it, in remembrance of me."

-1 Corinthians 11:24-25

His point was, whenever we do this, we remember Christ. I don't believe there is a black-and-white clear teaching that tells when. It is just something we should do as the body of Christ. And they were doing it.

Prayer

Then we see prayer capping off this short, but essential list of how the church functioned and focused and what we should model today. Probably my favorite example of prayer (there are so many examples, so where to begin?) is in Acts 4. Peter and John had been out doing what they were called to do—tell everyone about Jesus. The religious leaders of the day did not want to hear this message anymore and they didn't want to be challenged or convicted. So, they threatened the apostles to not teach about Jesus anymore. But the really cool and goosebumps part that would be the defining moment in a movie (I think in movies sometimes-ha!), is what they said and did when they went back to the other believers:

> Indeed Herod and Pontius Pilate met together with the Gentiles and the people of Israel in this city to conspire against your holy servant Jesus, whom you anointed. They did what your power and will had decided beforehand should happen. Now, Lord, consider their threats and enable your servants to speak your word with great boldness. Stretch out your hand to heal and

27

perform signs and wonders through the name of your holy servant Jesus." After they prayed, the place where they were meeting was shaken. And they were all filled with the Holy Spirit and spoke the word of God boldly.

-Acts 4:27-31

Prayer is not just some religious practice they did. It was their communication to God. I know that's a fairly obvious statement, but it's worth saying. This communication with God was not just something they did right before they ate their meal, or at the end of a sermon, or just when they needed the answers to a test they didn't study for. It was more than that. It was as real as me talking with someone face to face and expecting to hear from that person.

This is what is missing in our prayers today. At least, I know I haven't always approached prayer with that type of real and genuine belief. As I've been growing up in the faith and learning more and more about life in Christ, I've been drawn back to a simpler relationship to God that is driven by authentic prayer.

Here's what I know about real prayer from the Bible:

Prayer is the precursor to everything

Everything that has the backing of God and is any kind of God-mountain-moving event always has prayer as the precursor. It must start with prayer, or it's just our futile efforts. I've seen this many times in my sermons throughout the years. There have been numerous times where I studied like crazy, had perfectly timed witty statements, and well-thought-out relevant jokes (even this sentence sounds sermonesque), but no revival swept through the land. No salvations. Not even one tear when I delivered a great emotional story.

Then, on the other side, I delivered sermons I felt were not going to be accepted very well. I studied and prayed like crazy (sometimes because I felt totally unworthy and knowing I needed God's help, because it was tough), but the responses were polar opposites. I can clearly remember times when I was like, "Man I think my delivery was terrible. My jokes weren't any good and I forced them. They're probably going to be looking for a pastor next week." Haha!

But you know? I was looking at it as if everyone's decisions were based off my efforts to craft this amazing message. And in those services I see people respond and give their lives to Christ, or make some decision, or just talk about how God spoke to them in some powerful way. It's because it was all God and it had His backing and power behind it. It wasn't me.

Belief is essential

This seems as if it should go without saying, but I don't think the modern church has the same belief as the early church. Look at Jesus' half-brother's statement in James:

> If any of you lacks wisdom, you should ask God, who gives generously to all without finding fault, and it will be given to you. But when you ask, you must believe and not doubt, because the one who doubts is like a wave of the sea, blown and tossed by the wind. That person should not expect to receive anything from the Lord. Such a person is double-minded and unstable in all they do.

> -James 1:5-8

So we're told our demeanor toward God should be one in which we expect Him to respond to us. I'm always careful when I, in any way, refer to how anyone should expect God to do anything. God is not obligated to do anything. When I say this, I simply mean He is extremely generous with us and does respond to us. When He answers us, though, it is not always the answer we want. Sometimes His answer is "no" and sometimes it's "yes." But He is going to respond to us. That's what I mean. In a later chapter, I'll look more in depth at expectations with God.

Anyway, James gives us vital details about how we should approach prayer: believe and don't doubt. If we do doubt, we're given an explicit picture of what that looks like. He says we'll be like a wave in the sea that's just tossed around. Now think about that. I've been in the ocean. Each year we take people from our church to help with missions in Nicaragua. There is one particular beach that has these manmade dams that seem like giant sandbags. I'm giving a terrible illustration of what they are, but that is all I can do. So we would try our best to swim out to them as we struggled through the strong current. If we timed it just right and weren't completely worn out from the last time we tried, then we might be able to climb on top of one of them. So the goal was to get on top of it, wait for the huge wave to come over the dam, and take us with it. I remember a few times when I would go under the wave to try to get to the dam, but the wave would cause me to do flips under water with no control of my own. I was at the complete mercy of the water.

So if we compare that picture with what James tells us about being wishy washy in our faith, then we begin to see the utter futility of trying to hold to belief, yet unbelief. That's what we're doing. We're part of the way in with God, but then we say, "Well, wait, I'm not quite sure about this. This seems pretty crazy." And we go back and forth with no commitment whatsoever. We follow whoever has the coolest, most provocative new thing that day. We have no root or foundation. So James rightly says we shouldn't expect to receive anything.

Prayer is about God's will, not ours

Maybe that's harder for the American church to accept than the church in other places where they face real and physical persecution. I mean, let's just be honest about how it is here in the States for a minute. The problems we face in the church here are not so much about attacks against our freedom to worship. They're more internal, where we fight about the style of music; the type of church we'll be (contemporary, traditional, modern, classical, emerging, blah blah blah); or what the pastor says and wears. So I think it is more difficult for Christians in the U.S. to readily accept the idea of taking control out of our hands and submitting to God. The idea is repugnant to many.

Rather than spend more time stating what we probably already know about how hard it is to accept this, let's continue to look at Scripture:

> This is the confidence we have in approaching God: that if we ask anything according to his will, he hears us. And if we know that he hears us—whatever we ask—we know that we have what we asked of him.
>
> -1 John 5:14-15

By nature we want to leave out "according to his will." It just does not come natural to us in our flesh to want to do things according to God's will. That's why we sin, have issues, and are in this whole mess everyone finds themselves in. We want to do it our way and make everything about us. That's been getting us into trouble since the beginning.

So that's what I see about prayer in Acts and how the early church functioned. What was the result? Acts 2:47 tells us:

> "And the Lord added to their number daily those
> who were being saved."

-Acts 2:47

How amazing must it have been to be part of something that was so attractive, life-changing, and completely devoted to God?

Chapter 4
Zeroed in on the Mission

"The successful warrior is the average man,
with laser-like focus."

-Bruce Lee

There are times when I am studying for my next sermon and it goes really slow. If you're a pastor reading this, then you probably know what I'm talking about. Despite what you may think about pastors, we don't just step up on the stage; do the typical greeting; and then start talking, as the supernatural words that God wants us to speak over everyone comes out. No, we do actually study a lot, pray, and write and rewrite what we have learned and believe God is leading us to talk about. But there are times I approach a certain topic or scripture I had planned to discuss and it just doesn't flow the way I want. I read something, think about how to teach it, but then I'm led to other scriptures and feel as if I've spent so much time on trying to craft the perfect message to no avail.

But then I preach for weeks on a certain scripture, or topic, and it seems as if the sermon just writes itself. I have to cut stuff out, or add another week, because I could just get up there and start talking. Those are the times I have to watch the clock to make sure I don't talk so fast that I try to cram in everything that is bouncing around in my mind. Those are the times I feel as if I'm locked in and focused. There are just certain topics that I can talk about or write about endlessly because I am so passionate about the topics. Apologetics and evangelism are two areas where I don't need a lot of prep. I can just run with them. So it doesn't take much for me to be focused on those topics.

I like to be focused in my life because I get more done with a lot more efficiency and effectiveness. Isn't that how it is? Have you ever tried to be a multitasker? I've read tons of studies that assure us that no one can really be a multitasker. I mean, unless you know a scientist who is willing to clone you (we're still waiting on that to happen, right?) then you can only do one thing at a time.

Now everyone claims to be the exception to that. With the technology we have at the tips of our fingers, we think we've created a way we can do everything all at once, just like the woman who is late for work, flips the visor down, applies her makeup while steering with her knee, and eating a pop tart with her other hand. There is a great chance that something could go horribly wrong, or she's gonna look like a mess. Haha!

Here's where I think this relates to the American church in this day and time and to the generations coming up: if we try to do everything and be great at all things, then we're going to be vastly ineffective in the greatest calling. You see, the Great Commission is the mission that God has called His people, His church, to be all about in this world. Let's look at those passages from Matthew.

> Therefore go and make disciples of all nations, baptizing them in the name of the Father and of the Son and of the Holy Spirit, and teaching them to obey everything I have commanded you. And surely I am with you always, to the very end of the age."
>
> -Matthew 28:19-20

These are the exciting final words that Jesus left for us, His church, to do. I know some translations say, "teach" instead of "make disciples," but that's not the best way to translate this. In the Greek it translates to "make disciples," or "disciple." While teaching is part of that and is mentioned in verse 20, it does not exhaust the whole meaning. To be a disciple means a whole lot more. Webster's Dictionary defines *disciple* as "one who accepts and assists in spreading the doctrines of another."[1] So there is a time when someone needs to be educated in the teachings of Christianity. And that is part of what we should do as believers. But being a disciple and leading others to be disciples is more than just memorizing the scriptures.

When you read through the accounts of the early church in Acts, you see how they simply interacted with people and spread the message (as we saw in the definition of *disciple*) as they lived their daily lives. It seemed effortless. Don't get me wrong. I don't mean it was a cakewalk. In fact, it seemed as if they were persecuted around every corner, and most of them ended up giving their lives and in extremely gruesome ways. Read Hebrews 11 if you want to see how some of the early Christians were treated.

My point is I don't read anything about the early Christians getting together and saying, "Ok, so how do we fit this living for Christ into our daily lives? How do we live this out as we go along?" They may have had those conversations, but the only thing we read from them is their accounts of how they put life behind their faith.

We could go through Acts and see this played out. After the supernatural life-changing event that was the Day of Pentecost, the disciples just spread this message of hope through Jesus as they went about their daily lives. Chapter 3 begins with, "One day Peter and John were going up to the temple at the time of prayer...." That's exactly what I am talking about! "So this one day, just like any other, as the guys were going along, this amazing thing happened, as the disciples were simply being faithful." That's the idea. The picture we're given here is they just went about their lives normally and as the opportunities came their way, they seized them. Then Acts 5 gives us this powerful, overall picture of what their lives entailed.

> The apostles left the Sanhedrin, rejoicing because they had been counted worthy of suffering disgrace for the Name. Day after day, in the temple courts and from house to house, they never stopped teaching and proclaiming the good news that Jesus is the Messiah.

> -Acts 5:41-42

There is so much about these verses that is weird and foreign to most people today. I'll make an even more bold statement: these verses are weird, foreign, and out of place to most in the church today. Don't believe me? I'm not trying to say something that isn't true or make some outlandish statement just for effect. I've been in church for a while and that's my assessment based on what I see.

And, just so you don't think I'm shouting down from the peak of the High And Mighty Mountain, this has been missing in my life as well. That's what I've been working on: trying to be able to relate with their willingness to suffer for Christ. But seriously, how many of you hear this type of commitment and all-out devotion to God? How different would the church be if we could relate with these verses?

Now let me steer back to what the chapter was about: zeroing in on the mission. Let me remind you what the mission is. There is a lot to the church, but its primary mission is to make disciples. I'll confess to you my heart. I know many of you may be going through terrible relational issues, whether it is the possibility of divorce, dating problems, or trying to figure out how to raise your kids. I know some of you may be going through financial struggles. Maybe the word "struggles" massively understates what you're facing. I know some of you are even facing health problems that seem to have no possibility of you coming out with any hope for a long life.

Hear me on this because I don't mean it to sound harsh or callous: I don't care about those as much as I care about your salvation. I hope you accept that the way it is intended to come across. The most important thing is where we will be when we leave this world. That type of mentality is what drove the apostles and the early church, and it is the same mentality that must drive us as well.

Elisabeth Elliot said, "God's command 'Go ye, and preach the gospel to every creature' was the categorical imperative. The question of personal safety was wholly irrelevant."[2] I never see that on Christian bumper stickers. Maybe we as the church need to be drawn out of the shallow pool of selfishness and vanity. This isn't all about us. Living in this world is not just about us getting a better life, with a bigger house, and more toys so we can compete with our neighbors.

Maybe our life's mantra should change from "keeping up with the Jones'" to "reaching out to the Jones'."

So Christians, church, does that laser-focused mission of getting the gospel message out to whomever you possibly can drive you and your life or ministry? I have another thought that relates to this. I won't go too far down this rabbit trail (my wife would probably tell you my rabbit-trail journeys could get Siri lost). There is a relatively new phenomenon among Christians that they don't need to be part of a group of believers. People will commonly say something like, "I don't need to be part of a church to be a Christian. I can worship God on my own."

I understand what they are trying to say, but that's a flawed premise because to be a Christian is to be part of the worldwide church of God. The church is not a building and it's not a specific denomination. It is the people who are disciples of Christ. I have never read anywhere in the Bible or get any impression that the early church had this type of reclusive lifestyle. The church seemed to be together and as a family.

All right, I'll jump off that trail and come back. There was a point I was trying to make. When we as the church do evangelism, the model we're given is to do this together as the church. Right? We were given the gifts to build up the church, not to use on our own behind closed doors. They were meant for the edification of the whole body. In the same way, doing the mission of the church—the great commission—should be doing it together as a whole body. I'm not saying you have to take a cue from the Jehovah's Witnesses or the Mormons and go two by two. You can just be going about your life and have a one-on-one conversation with someone. You don't have to call your pastor or your friend who is better in those types of situations. We are all supposed to participate in this commission.

Here are some thoughts to take with this:

Use your weirdness

Here's the thing: you and I are created differently. I have a certain personality that will connect with people you may not be able to, with specific things I am good at that you might not be so good at. In fact, David reminds us all of the personal touches that God places on our lives.

> For you created my inmost being; you knit me together in my mother's womb.

> -Psalm 139:13

What an incredible thought that God knit us together in our mothers' wombs! So I wanted you to grasp the personal and intimate touch that God had in creating you. You and I are not an afterthought. We are not made in some general way on a conveyor belt. You are the way you are because God ordained it that way. So the most effective way we can be used by God to reach others and tell the world about Him is by honing the skills and personality He specifically gave us.

Now I'm not so arrogant to say that you and I are the ones who save people by our own abilities. No way. God is the one who saves people. That has to be understood. I am just pointing out how we can be used effectively the way God intends us to be.

So when I say "Use your weirdness," I mean use your personality, interests, and things God specifically made you passionate about to connect with people and lead them to Him.

Tell your story

This is the part where we say in the church to share your testimony. The Bible describes it this way:

> And this is the testimony: God has given us eternal life, and this life is in his Son. Whoever has the Son has life; whoever does not have the Son of God does not have life.

> -1 John 5:11-12

So you sharing your testimony (your story) is explaining how what is said in these verses became real in your life. Don't underestimate the story you have of how God changed your life. I am someone who loves apologetics and answering questions about God and the Bible. I love to get into deep topics about religion with people.

When I was first introduced to apologetics, I had to come to the realization that I could not completely knock down any doubts people may have that God exists. You know what I mean? I had to learn I couldn't make everyone believe in God because of my flawless arguments and quick answers.

There is definitely a place for arguments and intellectual answers that we can gain from apologetics, but the power of a personal testimony can knock down walls that answers sometimes can't. I have seen people connect with others in powerful ways when someone just opens his or her heart to them. There is just something about someone who is willing to be transparent about his or her life that removes barriers that people erect when referring to God.

Whenever I teach people how to share their story of faith, I always tell them to be able to tell the short and the long version of it. So if you are in line at the supermarket and happen to get into a conversation with the checker, pull out the short form. The people who might get in line behind you will most likely not appreciate you talking about your childhood, your family life growing up, all your good and bad experiences at church, and then finally your story of coming to Christ. You might inadvertently lead people to the bad side.

Know the gospel

This should go without saying. Right? I can't stress this one enough. It is not enough for us to simply be good speakers or be able to positively speak about how good God is. I'm not against that. We just have to be able to explain what it actually means to come to Christ. There is a passage from Matthew that scares me and drives me at the same time:

> Not everyone who says to me, 'Lord, Lord,' will enter the kingdom of heaven, but only the one who does the will of my Father who is in heaven. Many will say to me on that day, 'Lord, Lord, did we not prophesy in your name and in your name drive out demons and in your name perform many miracles?' Then I will tell them plainly, 'I never knew you. Away from me, you evildoers!'
>
> -Matthew 7:21-23

Those verses don't scare me because I question my stand with God. They scare me because I know there are countless people around me every single day who are in this number. But it also drives me to get the message of hope out to everyone I am given the chance to. The church is given the great commission. We are commissioned to get the gospel message to everyone in every place in this world.

So, Christian, that means you have an enormous responsibility to know what it is you believe and how to get that message to a lost and dying world. Part of that lost and dying world is across the street from you, across the cubicle from you, or across the living room from you. The great missionary Hudson Taylor said, "The Great Commission is not an option to be considered; it is a command to be obeyed."[3]

Chapter 5

Just Jesus

"Not only do we know God by Jesus Christ alone, but we know ourselves only by Jesus Christ. We know life and death only through Jesus Christ. Apart from Jesus Christ, we do not know what is our life, nor our death, nor God, nor ourselves."
-Blaise Pascal

This would be the perfect time to remind the church to KISS. You know? Keep it simple stupid. Right? I can't think of anytime it is beneficial to overcomplicate things. Whenever I counsel couples, I never tell them to hold in their feelings. I don't say, "If something is bothering you, don't bring it up with your spouse. Suppress those feelings as long as you can. And when your spouse does something, even when the spouse don't know he or she is doing something against you, push those feelings way down and just complicate the marriage. Everything always works out better when you keep your spouse on his or her toes, wondering what is wrong with you." That would be the most insane couples' advice anyone could receive.

So what can the church learn from that terrible couples' advice? We most definitely do not need to overcomplicate the gospel. I just read where another prosperity gospel pastor is asking for an exorbitant amount of money for his fourth "needed" private jet. I mean, I get it. I need multiple private jets like the next guy, but come on (that was sarcasm by the way). So we're doing a great enough job of complicating Christianity and what it means to follow Christ on our own. We can't, then, make the gospel message more difficult than it was intended to be.

If you have been to any church business meeting, or maybe even larger denominational meetings, then you may think there is nothing more time consuming, or boring, to be blunt. Now don't write me or send me hateful emails. I know that great good can come from them, and, to a certain extent, they are necessary. At least some of them are.

One such meeting happened way back in the early church. It was in Jerusalem and it addressed the changing culture of the church and how to respond to it. You see, the Gentiles were now coming into the church. For a long time, God's people were the Jews and those who adhered to the ways and customs of the Jewish people.

I really think some of them felt their nice, neat system was being infringed upon. Integration of anything, or any group of people, can be a daunting and unwanted task. So there was naturally some hesitation when Paul, Barnabas, and others brought the news that the Gentiles were being introduced into fellowship with the Jews. So the meeting was birthed:

> Certain people came down from Judea to Antioch and were teaching the believers: "Unless you are circumcised, according to the custom taught by Moses, you cannot be saved." This brought Paul and Barnabas into sharp dispute and debate with them. So Paul and Barnabas were appointed, along with some other believers, to go up to Jerusalem to see the apostles and elders about this question. The church sent them on their way, and as they traveled through Phoenicia and Samaria, they told how the Gentiles had been converted. This news made all the believers very glad. When they came to Jerusalem, they were welcomed by the church and the apostles and elders, to whom they reported everything God had done through them.
>
> Then some of the believers who belonged to the party of the Pharisees stood up and said, "The

Gentiles must be circumcised and required to keep the law of Moses."

-Acts 15:1-5

This would've been all over the news. Headlines would've flooded social media. *Church Split Inevitable! Can Jews and Gentiles Coexist (bumper stickers available)? One Group Suggests Peter Become The First Pope.* Some of these might be a little too real. Actually, though, this chapter provides some keen insights about how issues in the church should be handled and how we can have productive church meetings.

Ok, so they dismissed, discussed, debated (any other d words?) and finally reconvened to give their deliberation (I guess there was another d word). Their response had to do with the culture and what they were dealing with in that day and time. James, Jesus' half-brother, gave the response.

It is my judgment, therefore, that we should not make it difficult for the Gentiles who are turning to God. Instead we should write to them, telling them to abstain from food polluted by idols, from sexual immorality, from the meat of strangled animals and from blood. For the law of Moses has been preached in every city from

the earliest times and is read in the synagogues
on every Sabbath.

-Acts 15:19-21

What a perfectly controversial statement to make. This
is even debated in the present-day church. "How much of the
law do we need to do to be accepted by God?" "How does the
law relate to the message of Jesus?" "Is it really grace through
faith that saves us?"

I want to clarify what this is saying and not saying.
This is not saying, "We've had too many rules and it's been
pretty difficult for people to keep them. Let's whittle them
down to four." No way. These were not things required to be
saved and made right with God. In the next chapter, a jailor,
after he had just witnessed some amazing circumstances that
changed him, asked what he needed to do to be saved. Paul
simply responded to him in Acts 16:31, "Believe in the Lord
Jesus and you will be saved."

So that brings us to the title of this chapter, which is
"Just Jesus." Nothing more, nothing less. The church must not
complicate this or add to what the gospel is about. It is
salvation through Jesus alone. So if you are teaching a
message about salvation that includes Jesus plus something
else, then ultimately you don't have to worry about what I
think or say, but what you'll say to God. That's a scary
picture. Let me paint it for you with the words in Hebrews

10:31: "It is a dreadful thing to fall into the hands of the living God."

The early church was zeroed in on and passionately committed to teaching the message of "just Jesus." So my question for us today is, "Why would we change that in any way?" My favorite example of this unwavering commitment to Jesus alone was Paul. He wasn't only focused on teaching "just Jesus," but his message was very simple too. I don't mean that he wasn't deep and couldn't hold his own in a debate. I mean that he didn't clutter the message with unnecessary points.

The longer I have preached, the more I have learned this. I can go on all kinds of rabbit trails. My wife will point that out to me sometimes as well. "You were doing good here, Kyle, but then you drifted into this area and...I'm not sure why."

Their conversations seemed to have a plan and a map, which always led to Jesus. Look at what Paul said to the people of the Corinthian church:

> And so it was with me, brothers and sisters. When I came to you, I did not come with eloquence or human wisdom as I proclaimed to you the testimony about God. For I resolved to know nothing while I was with you except Jesus Christ and him crucified. I came to you in weakness with great fear and trembling. My message and my preaching were not with wise

and persuasive words, but with a demonstration of the Spirit's power, so that your faith might not rest on human wisdom, but on God's power.

-1 Corinthians 2:1-5

Paul had to address so much to this young and struggling church: divisions, immorality, false teachings, disorder, and misuse of spiritual gifts. But his comments to this church early on were his focused stance on making the message about Jesus alone. What does he mean by "For I resolved to know nothing while I was with you except Jesus Christ and Him crucified"? I really think we could spend the rest of this book talking about that type of commitment and what Paul was saying there. Right from the beginning Paul is saying he had made up his mind that he was going to be all about Christ and Him crucified. That was his life after his conversion and what he would teach from that point on.

Our compliant and non-committal culture has a tough time taking the hard-lined stance that Paul does here. This isn't popular. It's difficult. Many don't want to come to terms with the fact that believers are compelled to make a decision. We can't straddle the fence in our walk with Christ. Straddling a fence is not a comfortable feeling. Physically doing so is not a pleasant experience. Right? I don't need to paint the picture, do I? Joshua states the case as well as anyone:

But if serving the Lord seems undesirable to you, then choose for yourselves this day whom you will serve, whether the gods your ancestors served beyond the Euphrates, or the gods of the Amorites, in whose land you are living. But as for me and my household, we will serve the Lord.

-Joshua 24:15

This type of bold, make-a-real-decision attitude is uncommon now. Today we take verses like this and put them on pictures or rustic wood decorations and display them on our walls. I'm all for displaying scripture on our walls. You can come to my house and see us doing this. The problem, though, is that for too many, we have removed these scriptures from the context of what was being said and relegated them to vague and superficial statements. I'm afraid if some were pressed for an answer about what those scriptures really mean to them, they might simply say, "Oh we believe in God. We're on the Big Guy's side."

I encourage you to read the rest of that chapter. The conversation was a lot deeper than we make it by our decorations. The people essentially responded that they wouldn't turn from God and reminisced about how God had done amazing things through them and protected them. But look at what Joshua says, and, digging deeper, how he points out the seriousness of really committing to God:

> Joshua said to the people, "You are not able to serve the Lord. He is a holy God; he is a jealous God. He will not forgive your rebellion and your sins. If you forsake the Lord and serve foreign gods, he will turn and bring disaster on you and make an end of you, after he has been good to you." But the people said to Joshua, "No! We will serve the Lord."
>
> -Joshua 24:19-21

Do you get the context? He's like, "Do you guys really mean what you're saying? This is a serious thing. You can't simply say a meaningless statement and expect the holy and just God to accept you."

So with that in mind, I want to go back to Paul and his stance on Jesus alone. That's the background behind his decision. He's not making a general and politically correct statement to get likes on his feeds. His decision is well thought out and calculated. He is intentional in what he says and what he did.

I think he learned as he grew in Christ. I know I have as I've matured in my faith. There are things I was focused on when I was younger that I realize now are secondary, or even to be abandoned. It really is all about Jesus and Him crucified.

Paul understands this and deliberately constructs his whole ministry and life around that essential theme.

So let's talk about how that looks. I've read books and been in discussions in person and on social media about what this should look like in our daily lives. To keep this simplified, I just want to throw in my two cents on how much we should talk about Jesus, or how quickly we should move the conversation to Him. I know that probably sounds like I'm turning Jesus talk into a business, but that's not where I'm going to shift the discussion and I ask you not to let your mind wander to that either. I simply want to talk about the simplicity and straightforwardness of what we are about.

Why in the world (if we truly believe in Jesus and that He did come into this world, die for our sins, and rise again, giving us the way for our sins to be forgiven and a way to have eternal life by trusting in Him) would we keep that to ourselves? You get me on that? You and I and the church must come to terms with this. We have to wrestle with this and admit that too often we are weak when it comes to making our whole life about Jesus and Him crucified.

How Often Do We Talk About Jesus?

Let me make this clear right now: There is not some number I am shooting for, or a percentage I think we should hit. In many ways I am against all the church numbers that we're told we should hit to be successful, whatever that means. Many churches have hit all the "right numbers" and done everything on the checklist of what it takes to be the "next big thing." But the argument could be made that the church that "nailed it" according to the world's standards has totally "missed it" by God's standards.

So I take more of a fanatical stance on this. I think we should talk about Jesus and what He did all the time. Now let me be honest and upfront here. I am not anywhere near where I want to be in following this belief. So I am not putting myself out there as someone who has this down. I'm just another guy who's revealing what he sees as the model and stating this as his goal. All right? This is what I'm shooting for and what I push everyone else to shoot for as well.

The more I read Scripture, the more I see how these early believers shaped their whole lives around the reality of what Christ had done for them and that they were compelled to get that message out to as many as they could. So when I'm asked if it seems a little crazy and overzealous to want to use every single opportunity I can to lead someone to Christ and what He did, my only response is, "How can I not be obsessed with getting His message out?" Shouldn't we rather think it's strange to keep this powerful message to ourselves? Here's how I see it: I am going to be in heaven with God for all eternity. If I am going to a place forever, why wouldn't the One who made that possible consume my life now?

So I believe our conversations and relationships should be about Jesus. I'm not saying if you are talking about sports, or a movie, or a certain shirt to buy, that you have to draw those conversations around to Jesus every single time. I do believe, however, that we all have many more opportunities than we seem to think. A good litmus test on how well you make Christ all about your life is to see what others think or say about how you live and what is most important to you. Constructive criticism can be hard and revealing, but if we see it as an opportunity to grow, it changes everything.

So how do people see you? How would your coworker, your boss, your spouse, your kid, your neighbor, or even the coffee worker who knows your name and what you drink before you even say a word, describe the driving force in your life? Would they even know you followed Jesus? As I have just said, "How in the world can I not tell everyone who Jesus is and what He has done?" My goal is to make what Paul said my motto in life and ministry. "For I resolved to know nothing while I was with you except Jesus Christ and Him crucified."

Chapter 6

Love: Real; Genuine; Active

"If you live gladly to make others glad in God, your life will be hard, your risks will be high, and your joy will be full."
-John Piper

The greatest blunder in advertising (according to me, but I'm no marketing agent) is to create an ad that completely misses what you're trying to sell, or even repels your audience. Right? I mean the whole point of marketing is to get your product known and wanted by the masses. So if your marketing strategy misses the mark on your goal, it can be catastrophic to your sales. The key to getting people to like your product, idea, or whatever you are offering, is to make it appealing by putting the positive on display.

Those were just some thoughts I had while I was thinking about the early church and how their genuine, authentic love was on display for all to see. Their neighbors and acquaintances may have disagreed with their theology, but it had to be pretty tough to find fault with the way they loved each other and did life together. In fact, it was Jesus who introduced this type of genuine and attractive love. This is what He said to His disciples:

A new command I give you: Love one another. As I have loved you, so you must love one another. By this everyone will know that you are my disciples, if you love one another.

-John 13:34-35

If you haven't figured it out by now, love is a pretty significant piece in God's plan. At length God reminds us to an excessive degree that we should love. We just don't get it. But here's what I think is pretty cool. He says that people will know we're His—we're Christians—if we show this kind of love for each other. So that's what I really want the church to focus on.

Let me explain this before I really get into it. I am not saying we are to dress up the church, change it, and make it appealing only to people who don't go to church. That's where we're losing focus. Jesus is essentially saying, "Look, guys, just live the way I'm telling you, love each other the way I love you, and the world will know you belong to me and follow me." I think the world is actually massively intrigued, and even drawn in, by this unusual love. This sort of love is magnetic.

Look at a letter the Apostle Paul wrote to a young, struggling church in Corinth. Paul wrote to these people, answering many of their questions. But in one particular part, he gave an illustration of how the church is supposed to function. He explains the different gifts we are given and how that corresponds with the way the people—the church—are to relate to each other. It's one of my favorite pictures of how the church should look:

Just as a body, though one, has many parts, but all its many parts form one body, so it is with Christ. For we were all baptized by one Spirit so as to form one body—whether Jews or Gentiles, slave or free—and we were all given the one Spirit to drink. Even so the body is not made up of one part but of many.

Now if the foot should say, "Because I am not a hand, I do not belong to the body," it would not for that reason stop being part of the body. And if the ear should say, "Because I am not an eye, I do not belong to the body," it would not for that reason stop being part of the body. If the whole body were an eye, where would the sense of hearing be? If the whole body were an ear, where would the sense of smell be? But in fact God has placed the parts in the body, every one of them, just as he wanted them to be. If they were all one part, where would the body be? As it is, there are many parts, but one body.

The eye cannot say to the hand, "I don't need you!" And the head cannot say to the feet, "I don't need you!" On the contrary, those parts of the body that seem to be weaker are indispensable, and the parts that we think are less honorable we treat with special honor. And the parts that are unpresentable are treated with special modesty, while our presentable parts need no special treatment. But God has put the body together, giving greater honor to the parts that lacked it, so that there should be no division in the body, but that its parts should have equal concern for each other. If one part suffers, every part suffers with it; if one part is honored, every part rejoices with it.

-1 Corinthians 12:12-26

What a fantastic way to picture how the church should function! Right? I mean try to see the worldwide church as this fully functioning body that worked in complete harmony. If you've been a pastor for any amount of time, you've dismissed this idea altogether, though. But really, this is the picture we see from scripture.

When there is gossip in the church, it is like cancer beginning to form on a person's lungs. The individual may not know it is even there initially. In fact, he or she may be able to function without any hindrance for a while. But eventually, when the cancer begins to spread and grow, something must be done. Sometimes irreversible and life-threatening damage is done.

Isn't that the impression we're left with when talking about the church as a body? The church should be for each other and be functioning with a real purpose—living for God in every way. So love, as I already mentioned, is a huge piece of that. How do we function as a living body? How do we eliminate these life-draining and sinful tendencies we so often bow to? We do it through love. We love God and He does the transformation in us (Romans 12:2). He matures us and grows us and we learn how to love as He first loved us (1 John 4:19). Jesus says, therefore, "Love each other and get past these stupid things that are dividing you and causing unnecessary pain and problems. When you do this, people will get it and know that you follow me." I may have added a few words there, but that's what He is saying.

The greatest love chapter in the Bible (you know what it is if you've been to any wedding) is 1 Corinthians 13. That chapter is interesting because Paul begins to describe real love by describing life without it. I'm reminded of Scrooge being visited by the three ghosts who show him what his life is going to be like if he continues down the dark, lonely, and selfish road he was on. It wasn't a pretty picture.

Now he didn't really get it because he was in the middle of it, where we are so often blinded. So the ghosts gave him a life-changing opportunity to see his life from a new perspective. I remember the first time I recorded myself preaching and then listening to what I had said. I hated it! "I don't sound like that. Now I know why no one laughed at that joke." Have you ever been there?

There were parts where I was so sure I was speaking with so much energy and passion. When I watched it, however, I seemed monotone and dry. I flew through my jokes, which made me realize why I was the only one laughing. Trust me, if I would've delivered the sermon right, I would've brought the house down! At least that's what I tell myself.

In the first three verses, Paul reveals the absolute futility of a loveless life. In verse one he says, "It doesn't matter what language you speak; even if you can somehow speak the language of the angels, your life and words will still be pointless." Now remember, he was in the middle of a discussion on the gifts God gives us and how we should use those gifts. Many were abusing them and really just wanted recognition and adoration from others.

Some things don't change. So he says if you do this without love, it's like a really bad and annoying noise with no point. Don't think too hard about the meaning of the gong or cymbal (or however it may be stated in your preferred translation). He's just conjuring up the idea of a terrible, pointless, and maybe even painful noise. There was no rhythm or soothing sound coming out.

I think of a baby with two pots, just banging away. "Whose idea was it to give this kid these?" That's what our lives are if we don't have love.

Paul goes further with his illustration in verse two and, in my words, says, "Doesn't matter if you can prophesy (foretell future events or preach), have amazing Einstein-like knowledge, or Jedi-like, mountain-moving faith. Without love, you have nothing." Many try to make up for their lack of love. "Well, I may not be a loving person, but I bless the world with my enviable and unmatched wisdom." We are nothing without love.

Then finally, Paul goes into verse three and addresses those who may say, "I may not have love in my heart for anyone, but I will do the acts that are generally considered to be done by someone who has love. That's gotta count for something, right?" I am all for God's people stepping up, putting their money where their mouth is, and doing physical things to help others. We need to put our faith in action. That's what James so emphatically tells us. But it's more than just physically doing something. We must love.

Ok, so now we're back to the church and love. Love must be an integral part of everything we do. It must drive the way we live and be the reason we move to action. The rest of chapter 13 explains this love in detail. It is completely unselfish, unconditional, always moving forward toward the positive, and deflects any type of narcissistic self-centeredness.

So it's more than a simple statement. It's more than a step above the "like" stage. You know what I mean? "It's not you; it's me. I really like you. I just don't love you." Maybe you've heard that. Painful!

The love Paul describes here is one that will move you past a place where you don't mind being around someone. It is deeper than a relationship you have with someone you believe to be a pretty decent friend and you answer their calls without screening them. It's even stronger than the relationship you have with someone you consider to be in your inner circle.

This type of love is difficult because it makes us vulnerable and open. That's not a comfortable place to be in. No one wants to get hurt. So many times we put up these barriers and safeguards to keep us from being in the uncomfortable place. But the Godly example we're given is to knock down those walls and open up.

This isn't a prenup type of love. "I'm gonna release a little bit of me to you. But I'm gonna hold back this particular area, just in case something happens, or you do something." 1 Corinthians 13 seems to be all in. Jesus' love is all in. There are no such caveats we're presented with. This is what love is. Take it or leave it.

This is exactly the love the first Christians presented to the world around them. I can imagine the conversations that must've happened. "It's like they're not in it for themselves. I don't know if there is some hidden motive that I'm not getting here, but this is pretty impressive. How can I get in on this?"

Now that's just me throwing out those thoughts, but I gotta think it might be what some felt. I'm telling you, when unchurched people see the church come together and live out this Biblical, authentic, active love, it does something. I'm not foolishly going to say that people will automatically believe in God and start following Him. But I do think this type of love makes it a little harder for them to hold on to their opposing view.

Chapter 7

Eternal Focus

"Everybody wants to go to heaven, but nobody wants to die."
-Unknown

Do you remember *The Karate Kid* movie? The original one, not the remake with Jackie Chan. Mr. Myagi seemed to be getting lots of free labor out of Daniel. Daniel had come to him, wanting to be taught karate, but all Myagi seemed to leave for Daniel was a to-do list: paint the house, paint the fence, and wax and wash the cars. Pretty sneaky old man. Well played, Myagi. Well played. But when Daniel confronted him about it, do you remember what happened?

"Show me paint the fence!"

Then Daniel blocked a kick.

"Show me paint the house!"

Then Daniel blocked a punch.

"Show me wax on wax off!"

Then he blocked more punches.

Then Myagi just went off and kicked and punched, but Daniel blocked them all. Suspend your judgment for how believable that was to get the point. There was a reason Daniel was doing those chores.

Now, I could take this in another direction and speak about all the things God takes us through, or allows us to go through, because He is strengthening us and preparing us for the mission and opportunities He is planning to come our way. That is absolutely true. But I just want to speak about the truth that all the things we do here and the life we live for God is for a reason. There is something much better waiting for us. There is life beyond this life.

I have to admit, I'm excited about talking about what we'll be looking at in this chapter. It has to do with where we'll be for all eternity. It's such a cool topic. Now, I'm not looking at heaven in its entirety. I'm not going to develop an airtight case for heaven, what it will look like, and everything the Bible says on the subject. There are some great books out there that can help you understand that better.

I really want to single out some of the people and leaders of the early church to highlight the way they lived and discuss how their very lives confirmed they really did believe in heaven to tell you that this life is not all there is. But before we look at the way some of the early believers lived, let's look at Jesus' words to His disciples:

Do not let your hearts be troubled. You believe in God; believe also in me. My Father's house has many rooms; if that were not so, would I have told you that I am going there to prepare a place for you? And if I go and prepare a place for you, I will come back and take you to be with me that you also may be where I am.

-John 14:1-3

If you know any Christian music from the 90s, then you might be singing a popular song right now. That's an exciting message to get! "Don't lose hope, guys. This isn't the end of the line. There is a whole lot more."

Do you ever take some time and try and imagine, at least a little, about how amazing heaven is going to be with God? I think more Christians should take time to do that. Why not? Aren't we told to do this? Absolutely! Look at what Paul says to the church in Colossae:

Since, then, you have been raised with Christ, set your hearts on things above, where Christ is, seated at the right hand of God. Set your minds on things above, not on earthly things. For you died, and your life is now hidden with Christ in God. When Christ, who is your life, appears, then you also will appear with him in glory.

-Colossians 3:1-4

Because this amazing gift was given to you when you placed your faith in Jesus, take your mind off this world and put it on life with Him in heaven. When we give our lives to Christ, when we receive His gift of salvation, we have hope. We go from death to life (John 5:24). It's not hyperbole and He is not referring to joining a church social club in this world. We literally go from death to life. No, your physical body doesn't die right there and then come back in after a few seconds of flat lining. But spiritually we are brought to life through the work of Jesus on the cross and putting our faith in Him.

So yeah, the question should be posed, "Why would you continue to be distracted and weary by this world and what it offers?" It has no more influence on where you will spend eternity. Again, with the John 14 and Colossians passages in mind, we begin to understand what Jesus is trying to convey. "You have been changed. Your eternity is now set with Me and the Father because I am going to come back and get you to be with Me."

With that in mind, get excited and jump up and down, or whatever you do when you get excited. Let's take some time and put our hearts and minds on this place we're being told is not just hypothetical so we can try to manipulate our minds into being in a better mental state. We need to see that this is a real place (because it is) and to see that we are really going there.

Many people in the church seem more like closet skeptics. "I tell everyone I believe in all this heaven stuff and that Jesus is returning, but I don't really know. I can't express my doubts or ask any questions because I would be ostracized by my church."

I hope this is not the case for you, but if you have doubts, you gotta talk to someone and seek answers. God will show up.

Ok, so with all that in our minds, the attitude of Paul makes sense. If you don't know much about Paul before he began to follow Christ and become this stalwart for the faith, he was kind of a turd to Christians. Can I say turd there? I guess I just did. Anyway, Paul was aggressively going after Christians. He wasn't opposed only to those who followed Christ. He wasn't merely indifferent, or even open to civil debate. He was throwing them in prison and having them killed.

The only thing I can think of when I see people so radically changed is that they had to have really come into a real relationship with Jesus. Paul, after some time had gone by and he was boldly living for Christ, writes letters to churches while he is in custody. One particular letter he wrote to the Philippian believers. I'm encouraged and convicted by his faithfulness. Haha! You know what I mean?

Paul starts off the in typical fashion with the normal greetings and how he is praying for them. But then he says some crazy stuff you just don't hear from most Christians today. Essentially Paul says, "Hey, everyone, don't worry. Me getting thrown in prison is actually a good thing because the message of Christ is getting preached here. Not only that, but others outside these walls are getting encouraged to go even harder with confidence in sharing Christ" (Philippians 1:12-14).

Have you ever had a story of bravery that you were always recounting to other people? A defining story of your boldness you told to get recognition and adoration from people? A story you always kept in your back pocket and pulled out in those times when you wanted to be hoisted on people's shoulders (metaphorically of course)? Then you heard someone else's story and yours didn't have the punch you once thought? Haha! Right?

"I once caught a fish this big."

"Oh yeah? I used that as bait and caught one this big."

"Well...you're stupid."

Ha! I've never been there.

Paul was an opportunity seeker. He saw opportunities everywhere. He is in prison and is spewing out positivity. And then he says something that makes me stop and reread it every time. In Philippians 1:21 Paul says, "For to me, to live is Christ and to die is gain." That is a powerful statement. It is a verse I have highlighted in my Bible too because it must be something I learn to live by as well. I am pushing myself to be able to say that with as much passion and truthfulness as Paul does when he said this so many years ago.

As you read through this section, you get to feel the very real struggle that Paul has to be here or to go on and be with God in heaven. I mean seriously, I believe Paul is struggling with what he wants to do. "I so want to be done on this earth and go and be with God for all eternity. I cannot wait for this place. But...there is an enormous job in front of me. Everywhere I turn there are people who are lost and have no direction. They are on their way to an eternal destruction without God. I must do something."

That's what I picture from the words we have of Paul. Don't believe me? Look at his words:

> If I am to go on living in the body, this will mean fruitful labor for me. Yet what shall I choose? I don't know! I am torn between the two: I desire to depart and be with Christ, which is better by far; but it is more necessary for you that I remain in the body. Convinced of this, I know that I will remain, and I will continue with all of you for your progress and joy in the faith, so that through my being with you again your boasting in Christ Jesus will abound on account of me.
>
> -Philippians 1:22-26

First off, I have to acknowledge Paul's willingness to serve and reach people with the gospel. His pursuit was relentless. At one point in his letter to the Romans, Paul reveals his great pain and love for his people by saying he wished he could take their place at judgment (Romans 9:2-3).

I have thought about that a lot. Could I say that statement and truly mean it? I know a lot of Christians can get together and talk a big game and pretend our love is at this level. But if we're honest, I believe the number who are willing to do this for others is dramatically lower than we're led to believe.

I mention that about Paul to give us a sense of the real inner turmoil going on inside him. Paul's eternal destiny is firmly set. He knew he would one day—probably sooner than later—be in heaven with God. So when you weigh the options—stay or go—the obvious choice is to go to heaven. It is with God. It is perfection. There will be no pain, or suffering, or sin there. Why would you want to go anywhere else?

If you give a different answer, or conjure up some asinine alternate destiny, trying to sound smart, you are clearly misinformed about what heaven will be like. Simply stated, it is the best place and nothing even comes close. That is why Paul was ready to go immediately. As much as possible on this side of heaven, Paul had the correct view of heaven and eternal life with God.

Why then was it easy for him to know he needed to stay in this world? It was because, like I've mentioned in his amazing love, he knew God still had a mission to do through him in reaching people with the gospel. I've noticed something about myself. If I am going somewhere great for vacation, or I'm about to get off work for some time, then I am more willing to do some extra work or help someone out. You know what I mean?

I know this sounds selfish, but that is how I am. Now, don't get me wrong. I will still help people even when I don't have any time off. I will. But I know how much easier it is for me to be compassionate and to go out of my way to do some work for someone when I have something coming up to look forward to.

That may seem like an odd way to look at this, but I can picture Paul drawing the same conclusion. "I have the most amazing future waiting for me. So why would I not be willing to lay down everything for the sake of others?"

I don't want to leave it at that. There is a whole lot more going on in the mind of Paul than he was simply pumped about going to heaven, so he was ok with doing some ground work in reaching out to people with the gospel. I just want to clarify that. I do believe his excitement about this place—and the fact that he had faith that what God told him about it was something he could trust—it helped reinforce his hope and faith. But I can't get around the fact that he had this matter-of-fact attitude about heaven and that he was going there.

You know what that type of confidence does for you? It does two things:

You become overwhelmed with grace

First off, you are hit right in the face with a totally undeserved, unearned, and unbelievable grace from God. When you come to Jesus in faith, receive this forgiveness, and begin to understand what has truly happened to you, you cannot help but be overwhelmed by the goodness of God! This is one of those times when you are in a state of disbelief. "No. There's no way this is real. There is no way this can be happening to me. I am completely overcome with this love like nothing else I have ever felt before in my life!"

This is why people who have come to Jesus in faith are quick to point out how unworthy they are and that they don't deserve this gift. That's why Paul could say things like, "Christ Jesus came into the world to save sinners—of whom I am the worst." (1 Timothy 1:15)

I believe it is similar to that. You may think I'm exaggerating a little there. But if you comprehend that and reflect on what God has done for you, you can't help but be changed. This gives you a new way to look at life.

And secondly:

You gain a whole new perspective about life

You begin to see this world differently. Your priorities change. What you may have once thought to be insurmountable and life-draining begins to shrink. There are three times Paul wrote with this type of new perspective on life that encourage me. Look at what he says and mediate on this for your own life:

> I consider that our present sufferings are not worth comparing with the glory that will be revealed in us.
>
> -Romans 8:18

I could read more in that chapter and get lost in the amazing picture and description he is revealing about all creation, but verse 18 is enough for this conversation. It's a simple statement, but I think we can easily get it: "Don't lose focus in this world and whatever it is that you are going through. Nothing here can begin to compare with heaven and life with God later." Let's read more:

> For our light and momentary troubles are achieving for us an eternal glory that far outweighs them all. So we fix our eyes not on what is seen, but on what is unseen, since what is seen is temporary, but what is unseen is eternal.
>
> -2 Corinthians 4:17-18

In all honesty, it is usually hard for me to make it past "light and momentary troubles" and take Paul seriously. I say that because I know a lot of Paul's story. He went through more physical, spiritual, and emotional pain than I have ever begun to imagine. Maybe you're thinking the same thing. But try to accept that for a minute and just see again what he is saying. This world is not all there is. Even though you may be facing unenviable pain and separation from people, these are only temporary. There is eternal glory waiting for you.

I want you to take a second and try to absorb that as a fact. If you have faith In Jesus, whatever it is you are facing, have faced, or will face is minuscule compared to your inevitable entrance into eternal glory. I chose the word *inevitable*, because I want you to see this as an established fact for those who have faith.

The last text is just a great way to wrap up this section and show you the great lengths God has brought Paul from his old life to a new one committed to Christ at all costs:

But whatever were gains to me I now consider loss for the sake of Christ. What is more, I consider everything a loss because of the surpassing worth of knowing Christ Jesus my Lord, for whose sake I have lost all things. I consider them garbage, that I may gain Christ and be found in him, not having a righteousness of my own that comes from the law, but that which is through faith in Christ—the righteousness that comes from God on the basis of faith. I want to know Christ—yes, to know the power of his resurrection and participation in his sufferings, becoming like him in his death, and so, somehow, attaining to the resurrection from the dead.

Not that I have already obtained all this, or have already arrived at my goal, but I press on to take hold of that for which Christ Jesus took hold of me. Brothers and sisters, I do not consider myself yet to have taken hold of it. But one thing I do: Forgetting what is behind and straining toward what is ahead, I press on toward the goal to win the prize for which God has called me heavenward in Christ Jesus.

-Philippians 3:7-14

Whenever I read that I feel as if I have to put my fist in the air and say, "Yeah!" I don't if I'm reading it in public, though. I might get some weird stares. But don't you feel it? The passion, excitement, and sense of purpose in living in Christ. It's like a really great football coach giving the halftime speech of his life to a team that is on the verge of greatness, but just needed that little bit of reminding that they can do this.

Those of you in Christ, this is a pep talk from Paul. Press on! Don't look back! Trust Him above everything else! This world is not the end! You are not doing this for nothing!

One day you will be in the Paradise of all Paradises with the King of all Kings!

Chapter 8

On the Winning Team

"The early church didn't experience explosive growth in the face of relentless persecution for believing the resurrection was a metaphor."
-David D. Flowers

It's fun to watch pro teams learn they made it to the playoffs. Have you ever been watching a baseball game when that happens? The team is in the middle of a game that may have had some potential to affect the playoffs, but then another team loses and causes this team to be in no matter what. The team is excited and they start celebrating; however, there is still the matter of this game to be played. Some might look at it as if it's pointless and they should just call it.

But I see it another way. All the pressure is off. Now the game can be played for pure fun. The players can take all the risks they may have been too careful to chase had it been a must-win game. Now everyone is just free to play with no restraint. Swing a little harder at a pitch to try to get another homer. The game's not on the line, so why not? Take a huge lead at first instead of a more conservative one. If you get picked off, no big deal.

What if we had that same attitude and approach to life as followers of Christ? If you are a Christian, then you are on the winning team. Just like the baseball team who learned on the scoreboard that their rival lost, which automatically puts them in the playoffs, you too are assured of an eternal life with God in heaven. So why in the world would God's people take a conservative approach to life?

If you haven't gotten the clue in reading this far, I really want to push you completely out of your comfort zone into the great unknown with God. We are on the winning team. God wins. It's not a good possibility, or even a 99% probability. It is a 100% fact. If Christians would understand this, we should be living our lives with no regrets, no fears, and all-out trust and devotion to God.

Every time I read about the early church and dive into those powerful stories that are left behind for us to see, I never cease to be amazed. If you follow any church history and trends in the church, you're probably aware of the opinions about the state of the church. Everyone has an opinion. I am against us as believers trashing each other in public and on social media. I don't believe any good can come from us tearing other believers apart and gossiping about the different church down the street that is reaching a diverse crowd.

Having said that, I cannot deny there is something wrong in the church today. I can't argue against the idea that the church in America is unquestionably different than what I have read in Acts. So what is it? Well, that's what we've been discussing throughout this book.

What I see regarding their courage is that it undoubtedly points to a real belief in God. You know what I mean? The way they lived and some of the courage they displayed, that they shouldn't have had, reveals to me that they were all in on this. It confirms to me that they genuinely believed in God and had His Spirit working big time in their lives. It was God supernaturally working in and through them.

A few chapters back we looked at Acts 4 where the early believers were brought to a fork in the road. They had a big decision to make. Were they going to heed the demands of the religious leaders to stop telling people about Jesus, or was this going to force them to see how strong and authentic their faith really was by trusting in God even more? I am thrilled to read that they chose the latter and did not cave in and showed all of us a super simple, but powerful example of what to do in a similar situation. They prayed to God and they actually believed He would move. But that's the subject I'll speak about in the next chapter.

You know what I think they seemed to do really well that I don't always see today? They had a real faith. Like a real, mountain-moving, I-don't-know-what's-gonna-happen-when-I-take-this-next-step kind of faith. So I want to walk you through what I've found in Scripture. First, let's address this very simple, standoffish, non–committal counterfeit that is masquerading as authentic Christianity. That's a lot of adjectives, but trust me, I could have written many more.

So what did Jesus really ask of His followers? I'm not going to rehash the whole New Testament, but there are some words He said that I believe are extremely relevant for this very topic. They're not easy and can punch you in the gut pretty hard. Look at what He said:

> Large crowds were traveling with Jesus, and turning to them he said: "If anyone comes to me and does not hate father and mother, wife and children, brothers and sisters—yes, even their own life—such a person cannot be my disciple. And whoever does not carry their cross and follow me cannot be my disciple.
>
> -Luke 14:25-27

Mic drop. Man, this is extreme stuff here. Let's call it what it is. This is hard to accept. He does not change His message or give a condensed, easier message when there are more people. Right? Would He have said, "All right, I see John and Andrew are here and they brought their cousins and their families. They are messed up and have a tough time with authority, so I'd better give them the Jesus light message." No way!

I can see the people saying, "This is the guy I was telling you about. He's doing some crazy things and saying a lot of good stuff. Oh everyone be quiet! He's about to talk. Shh." Here's a challenge: read only the words of Jesus. I guarantee you will be shocked at how upfront, bold, and different He really was from what many say about Him today.

It seems almost popular for us Christians to talk casually about the spiritual battle that believers go through. We talk about it or post about it. But maybe you've noticed, like I have, that a lot of times when we come face to face with a personal, spiritual battle, we understand this is real and not metaphorical. "Wait. This is real? So you mean we weren't just describing some uncomfortable experiences in life and calling them spiritual battles?" Picture a soldier in battle saying to his commanding officer, "Can you believe they were shooting at me back there? I didn't sign up for this!" But that's exactly what we do in the church all the time. I just want you to be aware of this.

This is the first step in faith—believing this is real. Believing God and what He and His word say to us is that crucial first step. So when I see the early church's faith, this is what they were about. They had a real, tangible faith. They didn't just do lip service. Hebrews 11 gives a great picture of what this type of active faith looks like.

Now faith is the confidence in what we hope for and assurance about what we do not see.

-Hebrews 11:1

There are two important words in that sentence that we need to dissect that will help us understand faith: confidence and assurance. Now different words may be used in other translations, but the meaning is going to be the same. My translation says "confidence," but it's also translated "substance." It's the Greek word *"hupostasis."* A word everyone uses, right? Now stay with me on this because it is important to see why this is said the way it is. *Hupostasis* can be defined as "assurance, confidence, reality, or substance."

Let me read what I think is a great picture of what this word is and helps us understand faith: *The Vocabulary of the Greek Testament* reports its use as a legal term. It says it stands for "the whole body of documents bearing on the ownership of a person's property, deposited in archives, and forming the evidence of ownership." The book suggests the translation, "Faith is the title-deed of things hoped for." The Holy Spirit-energized act of faith, which a believer exercises in the Lord Jesus, is the title-deed that God puts in his hand, guaranteeing him the possession of the thing for which he trusted Him. In the case of this first-century Jew, his act of faith in the Messiah as High Priest would be the title-deed that God would give him, guaranteeing him the possession of the salvation for which he trusted God. Thus, he would have assurance.

In other words, "that which underlies what is apparent." Amplified a bit further, it is that which, though perhaps unseen, exists beneath and supports what is visible. It then has the sense of a foundation. Even as the foundation of a building is unseen, and the building above ground is visible, the foundation–the hupostasis–is nonetheless real, supporting the building. Hupostasis can be seen as the unseen support of that which is standing in clear view.[4]

Faith has an unseen foundation supporting it. Here's what I want to make clear in saying that: faith and belief are not necessarily interchangeable words. I want to make a distinction there that I think will help us. So that you don't think I'm just splitting hairs, let me read a verse to point this out.

> But someone will say, "You have faith; I have deeds." Show me your faith without deeds, and I will show you my faith by my deeds. You believe there is one God. Good! Even the demons believe that—and shudder.

-James 2:18-19

So this is huge and, you guys, we have to get this down. I want to say something really tough to hear. You can't just have an intellectual belief that there is a God or that Jesus really lived. That's not enough. You can agree with me that there is a God, Jesus came into this world, and maybe even believe it's true that Jesus died and rose again. It's not enough to just agree with some facts. There is a difference between faith and simple belief in facts. I want you to see this.

Here's a good way for you to see the difference in the two words. Belief is something that your mind is convinced of. There is a conviction based on your perceived facts. So our beliefs are things we are convinced of. And we come to those beliefs usually based on knowledge we've gained, information, or experience. So because of that, our beliefs can change. Right?

Faith, on the other hand, in my own words, can be described as belief + action + confidence = faith. So I want you to see they are related, just not interchangeable. It includes our beliefs, but it's bigger than that. Faith requires action. And if it doesn't move us to do something and actually take some kind of action, then it's not really faith. And that's what James argued for so strongly. He said in James 2:17 that, "faith by itself, if it is not accompanied by action, is dead." So that's the uncomfortable thing we need to learn about our supposed faith. If there is no action behind it and a confident assurance that pushes us to move on it, then we don't have faith at all. It's dead. If there is no substance behind it—no *hupostasis*—then it is not faith.

Look at this in a practical, visual way. I could say I have faith that this chair I'm sitting in would hold me. But until I get in it, my faith is dead, right? Or you could say, "I believe God could use me to speak to that person and help me say what needs to be said. But I am just a little worried. What if it doesn't work out? So I'm not going to step out there." Is that faith? There is no action behind it. There is no *hupostasis* that is setting a foundation and driving a visual picture of your faith. Ok, so faith is actively living out what we believe. Look further in Hebrews and see this explained for us:

> This is what the ancients were commended for. By faith we understand that the universe was formed at God's command, so that what is seen was not made out of what was visible.
>
> -Hebrews 11:2-3

He says this is what the ancients were commended for. He just gives us a little preface here about what he'll be talking about—the faithful people of the past. But I love how verse three is slipped in here to illustrate this faith. I'll admit I used to read over verse three really quick and not notice why it was put here. I mean, you know, it's important to talk about creation. I get it because it has to do with faith. But it's more than that.

We've been seeing that faith is more than just a mental assent, or agreement to some facts. It's a living, active belief that produces visible results. So with that in mind, think about him pointing out everything coming into being out of nothing. We're reminded of the most powerful picture of faith in action. The invisible, active, faith that is the foundation and driving force of our visible world.

Think about this: at least 95% of everything in creation we can't even see.[5] So that's why I now see that the illustration of God creating everything from nothing and what is unseen—to give us what is seen—is perfect for us to understand faith. Paul talks about this to the Corinthians:

> So we fix our eyes not on what is seen, but on what is unseen, since what is seen is temporary, but what is unseen is eternal.
>
> -2 Corinthians 4:18

Faith without works is dead—it's nothing. It's not faith. Real faith has a driving force behind it—a *hupostasis*—a substance. It's not merely an agreement to some factual statements. It is belief + action + confidence or evidence. And we get this type of faith from God who Himself is that driving force behind the visible.

Even Hebrews 10:22 speaks of this type of true faith and how we can have full assurance when we draw near to God with a sincere heart because that's what faith brings. There's a good picture of this type of faith that you trust even though you don't see. In one particular instance, in Jesus' early ministry, He tells Peter to throw his net out even though Peter had already done it with no results.

> When he had finished speaking, he said to Simon, "Put out into deep water, and let down

the nets for a catch." Simon answered, "Master, we've worked hard all night and haven't caught anything. But because you say so, I will let down the nets." When they had done so, they caught such a large number of fish that their nets began to break. So they signaled their partners in the other boat to come and help them, and they came and filled both boats so full that they began to sink.

-Luke 5:4-7

If you remember, at the end of John, we see Jesus on the shore when some of the disciples are fishing and they hadn't caught anything. Do you remember what He told them then? This is the second time He gives them Divine fishing advice. Cast the net on the other side of the boat. And they caught 153 fish. I don't think they even hesitated. True faith produces action because it is driven by this *hupostasis*, this foundation, this unseen substance. God is behind it.

When you get that—when you allow the reality of faith to grip you—it moves you to action. I don't believe you can even help it. You see, if you are a follower of Jesus, then you are on the winning team. Just let that sink in for a minute. You don't just have a good chance. You aren't playing really good odds. It is an assured fact. God wins! And by the amazing grace and love of God, by faith in Jesus, we are included on that winning team.

So you see, the early church was different from so many of our churches today. They got it. They understood it. They knew they were on the winning team. And because they understood this, they were moved to an unstoppable, active faith that transformed and changed the world. What would our culture look like now if we got this? What would your city look like if you got this?

Chapter 9

Great Expectations

"The primary limitation in life is our low expectations for ourselves and others. When we expect minimum results, that's usually what we get."
-John C. Maxwell

We just joined a new gym in town. One of the unique things about this particular gym is they have massage beds, tanning, and toning machines. The tanning wasn't really a draw for me (I'm content with my two-shaded farmer's tan), but I do like the massage bed and whatever this toning machine is.

Well, one day I asked to go into the toning machine. I had no idea what it would be like, so I had no expectations. I was just gonna go in and try it out. If it happened to be good, so be it. So I went in, pushed the start button, the left arrow twice (just like the worker said), and stood in this enclosed area, with bright lights and a fan above me for twelve minutes. It did nothing for me!

I talked with the workers after and found out I was supposed to pick my level and then the floor would vibrate and give me some kind of workout. So, ashamedly, I admitted I wasted my time—for twelve minutes. But since I had no expectations in the beginning, I wasn't looking for anything special to happen.

In that same line of thinking, I know people who don't make New Year's resolutions because they don't want to fail to keep them. Makes sense. Their logic is pretty airtight. "If I don't shoot for anything, or expect anything, then I can never be let down." That last line just gave me a killer idea for a can't-miss dating book!

Let me remind you again what led me to write this book. This is what I said in the beginning. What I read and see in the New Testament is not what I see in Christianity and the church today. I know I am not alone in that conviction either. Anytime there is a sexual or physical harassment crime committed by a person, or group of persons on multiple people, have you noticed what happens? Most of the time the ones who were offended stay silent until one person speaks up. Then they feel empowered, or safe, to come out in the open.

That's the same type of movement I see happening in the church today. Some people are examining the Scriptures and are coming to the right conclusion that something is wrong and someone needs to stand up and be the voice. And doing so inevitably causes others to express the same convictions. Once that threshold is crossed, it shows others they can cross through that doorway as well.

I bring that back up again to try to draw you to where I am going. There are some very clear distinctions in a great deal of the church today from where the New Testament church was. Another one of those distinctions is the expectations of the believers then from many believers today. Let me confess something here. For most of my time in ministry, I have felt guilty for having any type of expectations from God. I want to clarify what I mean because I don't want to put a thought in your mind that is unintentional. I, in no way, believe God is obligated to do anything for you simply because Kyle wrote a book with a chapter about great expectations. I am not advocating for a me-centered, false prosperity message here. What I am saying is that our faith that God can do what He says and will do what He says seems to be lacking at best.

Let's talk a little about expectations and whether the Bible really says anything about that. I don't want you to think I'm just throwing out some unwarranted claim because I want to raise up some emotional feeling in you. We should always confirm with the words of scripture. That's what Paul commended the people of Berea for doing, right? Paul spoke of creation itself waiting in expectation for redemption.

I consider that our present sufferings are not
worth comparing with the glory that will be

revealed in us. For the creation waits in eager expectation for the children of God to be revealed.

-Romans 8:18-19

There's a lot to look forward to, but there are also expectations of judgment, which is reflected in Hebrews:

If we deliberately keep on sinning after we have received the knowledge of the truth, no sacrifice for sins is left, but only a fearful expectation of judgment and of raging fire that will consume the enemies of God.

-Hebrews 10:26-27

There are expectations throughout the Bible—good and bad ones, depending on our relationship with God. So let's talk about our role with expectations toward God. If you're like I was when I was younger and didn't expect anything, then you need to read James' words with me.

Consider it pure joy, my brothers and sisters, whenever you face trials of many kinds, because you know that the testing of your faith produces perseverance. Let perseverance finish its work so that you may be mature and complete, not lacking anything. If any of you lacks wisdom, you should ask God, who gives generously to all without finding fault, and it will be given to you. But when you ask, you must believe and not doubt, because the one who doubts is like a wave of the sea, blown and tossed by the wind. That person should not expect to receive anything from the Lord. Such a person is double-minded and unstable in all they do.

-James 1:2-8

Really assess what is being said there. Yes, God is sovereign and can do what He wants to do. Yes, God is not controlled by any of us. But there is definitely a condition placed on receiving answers from God. And it has to do with our expectations. When you talk to God in prayer, do you expect to hear from Him? That's a legitimate question. Your answer to that affects your whole relationship with God.

Look at what James says in verses five through seven. You, the believer, are told to ask God for wisdom, but you have to believe, or you shouldn't expect anything. So there's a stipulation placed on hearing from God. We must believe, or as James says, we're like "a wave of the sea, blown and tossed by the wind." Don't expect anything if that is you.

I am at a place in my walk with Christ where I am done coming to verses like this and stating something stupid like, "Well, look, what that verse really means is…" No no no!

What it really means is if you don't have faith and don't believe, then you're going to continue to see nothing happen and not receive answers from God.

Do you see something different than I do when you read that? Church, Christians, we have to stop coming to scriptures like this and reworking them to make them more acceptable and easier for the masses to get on board. We shouldn't add to scripture, or make it more difficult for people to understand, or be able to follow. We must raise our view of it, however. We have to elevate our position when it comes to interpreting and following the Bible.

Here's a question: "Where do our expectations come from?" Or more specifically, how would you explain to someone where your expectations of God come from? Have you ever thought about that? I hadn't, honestly, until I wrote this chapter. Follow me on this. Your expectations stem from your experiences. Don't they? I expect the sun to rise tomorrow with pretty much a 100% certainty. That's based on my experience of seeing the sun rise every day of my whole life, in addition to everyone I know, or have read about, seeing it as well. So I don't even think about that one.

I have a pretty high expectation that I will wake up tomorrow as well. This one's a little different, though. I also know there is a chance I may not wake up. I have always woken up before. I have never experienced not waking up, or this chapter would not have been finished. What makes this one different, however, is there is also evidence that everyone will die at some time.

I have some smaller expectations too. I expect my daughter to do what I tell her to do. Now this might be a little trickier, but there are still expectations. She may not do it right away (this seems to be the norm the older she gets), but I know she will eventually do it, based on the fact that she is a good kid and usually listens. I also have good expectations because I know we will punish her and make her do it if she chooses unwisely. Can I get an amen from the parents' section?

Now, where am I going with this? Your expectations regarding God and what He will or will not do are based on your experience with Him. If you are reading this and you are militantly against God, or there being a God, then your expectations of Him and His working will not only be low, but non-existent. On the other hand, if you are completely sold out to Him and follow Him with your whole being, your expectations are going to be high. Right? I think that's a pretty simple concept to get.

So in summary, your expectations are directly influenced by your relationship with God. If you have faith in Him, you will know Him. If you know Him, you will have the Holy Spirit. If you have this relationship with God that comes through faith alone in Jesus alone, then you will experience God in your life. So I would argue that your level of expectation regarding God and what He can, or will do, starts at this beginning stage of coming to believe and trust in Jesus by faith.

This is the beginning level. You could call someone a baby Christian here. That's not a foreign term in the Bible.

Paul wrote a few letters to the Corinthian church because of its numerous issues. Look at what he said about where they were:

> Brothers and sisters, I could not address you as people who live by the Spirit but as people who are still worldly—mere infants in Christ. I gave you milk, not solid food, for you were not yet ready for it. Indeed, you are still not ready.

> -1 Corinthians 3:1-2

There are levels of maturity in the church. Again, that is not something you haven't heard. But it's essential to know and to evaluate where we are as individuals in the church and where the church is as a whole. I am fully convinced the first-century church that I read about in Acts was looking at this world through a different lens than we do now.

I put on a buddy of mine's glasses one time. He has really bad eyesight. I mean seriously, these things could take a bullet. I wear contacts, but my sight isn't that bad. So I put his impenetrable eye protective gear/glasses on and everything was different. I could make out some images, but it was like smearing a thick coat of Vaseline on a window and attempting to describe what I saw.

But when I took them off and put in my contacts, I could see with much more precision. Everything became clear. I wasn't fumbling around, or reaching out slowly for something on the counter, or to turn on a light switch.

That's the type of disparity I see between the first century and now. So my battle cry with expectations is we need to change our lens. How the church sees God, what He is asking of us, and how we should relate to Him must change and be brought into focus. So if our expectations change, we will see God move in a much more visible and powerful way in our lives once we get our focus on Him, where it needs to be. It's like getting our eyes dilated. Ok, I'll stop with the eye illustrations.

Let's make this a little simpler and more practical for us to comprehend and then begin to do. We see that the early church looked at scripture and living a Godly life differently than a wide percentage of people do today. In other words, we must change our perspective. Your expectations with God and His activity in your life comes down to your experience with Him, which hinges on your relationship with Him.

So let's move from being infants in Christ to adults. There is a time to be in every stage of our walks with Him. There is a time when we are infants and we have to take on simpler things, soak everything up, and just sit and learn. But there is also a time to grow up.

In chapter eight I talked more in depth about faith and what it is. Reread that chapter to understand faith more so you can see its place here and how it influences your expectations. Real, authentic faith has a substance to it that drives what you do. In this case, you read the Bible and it talks about having a faith that asks God to give wisdom and to show up, and you believe that. In fact, what you do reveals that.

What good is it, my brothers and sisters, if
someone claims to have faith but has no deeds?
Can such faith save them? Suppose a brother or
a sister is without clothes and daily food. If one
of you says to them, "Go in peace; keep warm
and well fed," but does nothing about their
physical needs, what good is it? In the same
way, faith by itself, if it is not accompanied by
action, is dead.

But someone will say, "You have faith; I have
deeds."

Show me your faith without deeds, and I will
show you my faith by my deeds. You believe
that there is one God. Good! Even the demons
believe that—and shudder.

-James 2:14-19

Real faith that God is going to show up, move, give
wisdom, and do His thing is based on a faith that is not just lip
service. No, it is based on something that has a real foundation
to it. It is based on an active faith that moves you. The
alternative to that kind of faith...is demons! Seriously! He
compares dead, inactive, non-expectant faith that you and I

may have to Satan's guys. That's a terrible place to land, in case you didn't catch that.

So how do you view God? How do you look at His activity in the world and in your life? How do you look at His word and some of the crazy, unusual, and just plain extraordinary things He asks of His followers? We'll look at that in the next chapter.

Chapter 10
Stop Just Reading It!

"The Bible is very easy to understand. But we Christians are a bunch of scheming swindlers. We pretend to be unable to understand it because we know very well that the minute we understand, we are obliged to act accordingly."
-Soren Kierkegaard

One of the most pointless things is to receive information that is truly helpful and do nothing with it. You know what I mean? If, for instance, you went to the doctor for a check-up and you were told you had, I don't know, a 100% chance of growing a green arm out of your chest unless you took medicine (I'm a pastor, not a doctor. Stay with me), what would you do? I mean, after you told your friends and family about this weird predicament you are now in, you would quickly begin your new regimen for whatever crazy, no doubt, groundbreaking new disease this is. Unless you're trying to crack into the circus world with a new act, I gotta believe you are going to take the medicine.

In the same way, what if everyone decided that all the laws were really just suggestions? What if we all merely picked and chose whatever we thought we could follow? When I was sixteen, my mom was letting me drive her car. I had come from the bank and I remember passing one of the school buses. So naturally I sped up, hoping there was a slight chance that someone would see me driving and obviously realize I was cooler than they were. Well, as I passed them, a cop pulled up behind me, threw on his lights, and made me pull over. Not exactly the cool moment I had pictured in my mind, especially as I'm driving my mom's four-door Buick.

I have a few other stories in this car too, but that's not the point. Now this is where I was coming from in this upcoming conversation I was about to have with this policeman: my mom had previously told me she usually does nine miles over the speed limit and they usually don't get her. So when he asked me why I was going so fast, I had a Bobby Bouche moment. "Well, Momma said...."

The response I received back was, "Well, Momma's wrong."

So I took my ticket and didn't feel as cool, or as knowledgeable, about the world of driving.

My point here with the Bible is too often I see people reading the words, but it goes no further than that. They see the words and maybe even memorize them, or maybe even have them permanently tattooed on themselves, but they never do what it says. So here's the big point, the part where you pull out the highlighter and let it do its thing. If you get anything in this chapter, get this:

Read the Bible and do what it says

Honestly I could stop right there and that would be enough. It's seems so simple. It seems like I shouldn't even have to say this. What a novel concept, right? If you could take anything from this book, I believe it's this: just read God's word and do what He says. Check me and question me and all my thoughts. That's ok. In fact, you should check everything I say and make sure it's right and it lines up with God's word because if you don't, if you just hear from me and take everything I say as indisputable fact, then you could be deceived.

Don't worry, I'm not steering you wrong. This is an absolute necessity for Christians to do. Check everything out and make sure it is in agreement with God's word. Not enough people in the church are doing that now. I am convinced that is a huge reason why so many are being duped into doing immoral and unbiblical things in their so-called churches, with their so-called pastors and leaders.

We could talk about that for a while, but I want to get back to the big issue of doing what the Bible says. Look at what Jesus' half-brother James says because he uses a great illustration to help us comprehend this:

> Do not merely listen to the word, and so deceive yourselves. Do what it says. Anyone who listens to the word but does not do what it says is like someone who looks at his face in a mirror and, after looking at himself, goes away and immediately forgets what he looks like. But whoever looks intently into the perfect law that gives freedom, and continues in it—not forgetting what they have heard, but doing it— they will be blessed in what they do.
>
> -James 1:22-25

First off, this letter that James wrote is one of my favorites. It's so practical, hard hitting, and right to the point. And it's all about action. His words in this letter should be a smack-in-the-face, wake-up call for Christians and the church. Stop talking about doing something. Stop throwing your hands up in the air when the pastor says something convicting and giving him an "Uh huh. Preach it, pastor." Take the active step of faith and do what God is telling us to do through His word. Right? I can't even imagine how different the church would be if Christians would take the Bible seriously and actually follow it.

So back to James' words—what is he saying? The point is to not just hear or even read the words of Scripture, but to do what it says. So he uses an interesting analogy to illustrate this: a mirror. The picture is someone looking at a mirror. What's the point of a mirror? It shows us what is really going on with our looks. When I go to the gym, I feel as if I've stepped into a vanity fair. I mean, I can't really say anything; I usually try to flex in every mirror I see myself in.

The mirror really has one job and it is to reveal what you really look like. You can walk around with blinders on, never looking at a mirror, and pretend to be something you're not. I see some of the guys in the gym, flexing unashamedly in weird positions, trying to highlight the muscles they think they have. They're not taking the mirror's advice and hitting more weights instead of staring at themselves.

I can wake up in the morning and pretend I look presentable to the world even though I have bed head and bed beard (that's a thing). When I decide to check myself in a mirror, however, the truth has a different view. So at that point when the mirror shows my flaws, I have a choice: I can take its advice and fix the flaws it is showing me, or I can turn away from it and choose to forget what it revealed.

That is the analogy James is drawing between God's word and us. The point is, the Bible has the truth. It will reveal some things about us that we may not like. It often highlights areas in our lives that need to be changed, developed more, or just completely removed. Practically, this is how it looks. You come into church on any given Sunday and hear a message from the pastor. It's just a regular day at church. Music was good; the message was good. Nothing was great, though.

If we're ranking this on a baseball scale, it was a single to right. No homerun. There was only one amen and I didn't get an emotional high where I felt as if I could take out the next Goliath. But it was solid, and it was Biblical, and it addressed something in my life that I didn't want to deal with. It made me uncomfortable. Welcome to conviction! Where the temperature is never right and squirming in your seat is highly encouraged. Maybe we need more of this. Just a thought.

So what do you do in those moments? Because there are times when you will come face to face with convicting passages. You will be shown things about yourself that make you uncomfortable. You will be faced with the decision of whether you will look deeper into God's word, or step away from it, like you would from a mirror that gave you a less-than-desirable view of your appearance.

So are we going to do what God's word says we should do? You don't have to have a degree to answer that question. It's not a loaded question either. It is simple. Obey God, or do your own thing. There are no hidden motives. We all have to make a decision one way or another.

Have you ever heard of Occam's razor? It states that "principles employed to explain any phenomenon should not be multiplied without necessity."[6] All right, let's apply that principle to our reading of the Bible. Instead of just getting together, reading some verses, and trying to impress each other with how quickly we can cross reference each verse with another verse, why don't we also do what it says?

Don't complicate this process. God's word shows us what we should do; then the natural, easy thing to do is take the steps toward obeying. I didn't say getting together and having Bible studies is wrong; I said don't just read it. That's the first step. The next step is to actually do what it says. Be active! James goes into more detail:

> What good is it, my brothers and sisters, if someone claims to have faith but has no deeds? Can such faith save them? Suppose a brother or a sister is without clothes and daily food. If one of you says to them, "Go in peace; keep warm and well fed," but does nothing about their physical needs, what good is it? In the same way, faith by itself, if it is not accompanied by action, is dead.

> But someone will say, "You have faith; I have deeds."

> Show me your faith without deeds, and I will show you my faith by my deeds. You believe

that there is one God. Good! Even the demons
believe that—and shudder.

-James 2:14-19

I referred to these verses from James last chapter. I
love these verses because they get right to the issue of taking
action. I'm not saying I'm not equally convicted, though. I
am. I can fall into the hypocritical crowd and cheer loudly
from the bench and say "amen!" The point, though, is for us to
stop talking and cheering from the sidelines and get in the
game. What good is it church if we continue to yell from the
stands and act as if we have it all together, but we don't
actually do anything? It does nothing. We might make a lot of
noise, but is that the goal?

> Therefore, since the promise of entering his rest
> still stands, let us be careful that none of you be
> found to have fallen short of it. For we also have
> had the good news proclaimed to us, just as they
> did; but the message they heard was of no value
> to them, because they did not share the faith of
> those who obeyed.

-Hebrews 4:1-2

I could go to a huge conference, speak to thousands of
people, strategically say the right stories at the right times,

throw in an emotional story here and there like a sprinkle of salt for flavor, and have the audience at just the right emotional level. Then, what if I end the talk with the knock-out punch that it was all leading up to: the church must change? Can you picture it? I start getting the audience chanting it. I could even get it going like I was at the World Series and have a wave of this phrase echoing throughout the stands, everyone emotionally and emphatically saying, "The church must change!"

But then the conference is over, everyone gets out of their seats, heads to their cars, and goes home. Nothing changed other than most people got some goosebumps on their arms and had a moment. That might come across as a vast over-exaggeration, but I'm fairly convinced that is a typical Sunday experience for far too many people today.

I am completely past that superficiality and am craving more. I pray that whomever you are, you are sensing that same uneasiness and insatiable desire for more of Christ. Not a really cool building with the latest tech gadgets and innovations that can keep the attention of any teen, or focused-challenged adult, like myself, busy for hours. Not just a budget that could feed a small country. But a group of people who are so passionately and deeply in love with the Creator of the universe, that their lives and actions are indelibly affected by His words. We have to move past merely reading the words on the pages of the Bible.

Have you ever looked at the magic 3-D pictures where the image comes out at you? Some of you may have never experienced seeing those images come at you if those pictures don't work for you. People can be driven to some very angry places if everyone around them sees the picture flying out at them and they can't.

We should take a similar approach to reading God's word. We don't just glance at it in passing or quickly read a few sentences here and there. There is a deep meditation and study that goes into it. And then comes the beneficial part: His truth comes out to us. We start to grow and understand what it means to be a follower of Christ. And listen to me here: All this comes when we move beyond a shallow approach to reading scripture. I want to bring up James' words again here:

> Do not merely listen to the word, and so deceive yourselves. Do what it says.

-James 1:22

Chapter 11

I Have To Tell Everyone

"Have you no wish for others to be saved? Then you're not saved yourself, be sure of that!"
— *Charles Haddon Spurgeon*

"If you had the cure to cancer wouldn't you share it? ... You have the cure to death ... get out there and share it."
—*Kirk Cameron*

A few years ago my daughter played in a soccer league. It wasn't a competitive league and we knew it, but she wanted to play. She ended up having fun, except for the fact that no one in the league kept score. So whenever she made a score, it didn't matter because the kids were just playing the game for fun. I kept score, though. Whenever someone asked how it was going, I made sure to say what the actual score was and that we were winning (if we were winning). If we weren't, then it was just for fun.

We're in the pathetic age of participation trophies. That's like a cuss word to a competitive person. These participation trophies are birthed out of this politically correct society we now live in. You can't say anything, have an original idea, or adopt any sort of opposing view to the acceptable norm. Relativism is the new acceptable view. You believe what you believe, fine. Just don't push your views on me. As a result of this, we have become soft and fearful to express what we believe to be true. That weak stance becomes a huge burden to the commission that Jesus left His church to "go and make disciples of all nations."

"Well, what do you mean by that, Jesus? There are many other views out there that we have no business intruding on. Can't we just say you are a possible way that people could choose, but not force it on them?"

I think my daughter is going to be a hostage negotiator, or an international negotiator of some kind one day. There have been many times we've asked her to do some chores and she came back with her negotiation tactic and a possible compromise with the hopes of pleasing all parties involved. My wife's like, "No we told you to…," but I cut her off.

"Now hold on, let's at least hear the demands and… wait! No, do what you're told!"

I'm kind of slow. I'll admit. I'm learning to defer to my wife's judgments on some of my daughter's requests.

But think about it. Don't we try the same methods with God? "Ok, God, I see your list of demands and requests about how to be in relationship with you and how you want us to interact with the world. Now what are the top five that are a must for you and which ones can we leave off?"

So, Jesus, just before He left, told the disciples to go to everyone, tell them about Him, and make more disciples:

> Therefore go and make disciples of all nations, baptizing them in the name of the Father and of the Son and of the Holy Spirit, and teaching them to obey everything I have commanded you. And surely I am with you always, to the very end of the age."
>
> -Matthew 28:19-20

A few years back, famed magician/comedian Penn Jillette did a Youtube video that talked about an encounter he had with a Christian after one of his shows. He goes on to talk about this man and how he gave Jillette a New Testament Bible and attempted to lead him to Christ. He was impressed with the guy and was thankful for his willingness to do that. Now the really convicting part was what Jillette was almost prophetically saying to Christians. He didn't convert and he didn't change, but he said something that believers need to hear:

> "I've always said that I don't respect people who don't proselytize. I don't respect that at all. If you believe that there's a heaven and a hell, and people could be going to hell or not getting eternal life, and you think that it's not really worth telling them this because it would make it socially awkward—and atheists who think people shouldn't proselytize and who say just leave me alone and keep your religion to yourself—how much do you have to hate somebody to not proselytize? How much do you have to hate somebody to believe everlasting life is possible and not tell them that?
>
> "I mean, if I believed, beyond the shadow of a doubt, that a truck was coming at you, and you didn't believe that truck was bearing down on you, there is a certain point where I tackle you. And this is more important than that."[7]

Every time I read that I have two thoughts: conviction and compassion. I wasn't trying to alliterate there. Jillette's words are painfully convicting to me, especially to someone like myself who claims to love talking to as many people, or strangers, as possible about Jesus. I do not take near the opportunities I wish I did.

Now let me address what people in ministry are tempted to say here, just as I am: "He's just exaggerating here. I don't hate anyone." That may be so. You may not have a hatred for people who don't know or believe in God. But don't miss the headline here. If we do believe in Jesus and His words, then why aren't we telling everyone? Shouldn't we have an insatiable, unquenchable drive to get the gospel out? Shouldn't we want to do that until every single last person on this planet has heard and probably heard multiple times?

But we don't because our fear of rejection is stronger. Most people want social acceptance over gospel declaration.

We want social acceptance over gospel declaration

We should listen to the wisdom from Proverbs.

Fear of man will prove to be a snare, but whoever trusts in the Lord is kept safe.

-Proverbs 29:25

You want my humble opinion of why we listen to people and care about what they think more than God? We are way too near-sighted and lacking in faith. Even more simply stated, we literally see people; therefore, it's easier to give them more credence than the Almighty Creator. At least that's

121

the way I see it. The church today, to make a real lasting impact on this world, must get back that first-century passion.

Do you remember Peter and John in Acts 4 when they went before the Sanhedrin? "As for us, we cannot help speaking about what we have seen and heard." They were compelled! Have you ever been so moved by something that it was impossible for you not to do something? I don't mean like a Girl Scout comes to your door with cookies and you are so moved by the presentation of the cookies on the box that you had to buy.

The type of movement I'm referring to here is one that causes you to push past your fears and uncomfortable feelings that previously held you captive. You have a different perspective now and those past fears and uncomfortable things that once seemed enormous are now small and insignificant in light of your different vantage point. You are now compelled to move as if something outside you is pushing you.

Speaking of compelled, there are a few instances where Paul used the word *compelled* to get the gospel out:

> "And now, compelled by the Spirit, I am going to Jerusalem, not knowing what will happen to me there. I only know that in every city the Holy Spirit warns me that prison and hardships are facing me. However, I consider my life worth nothing to me; my only aim is to finish the race and complete the task the Lord Jesus

has given me—the task of testifying to the good news of God's grace.

-Acts 20:22-24

Paul is giving his farewell message to the Ephesian Elders—people he loved and served with. He's being very candid about what he believes he will go through. He is going into this with his eyes wide open, with complete awareness of the dangers. Through all this, however, his whole aim and purpose is to be obedient to God and spread the only message that can bring hope and salvation to the world. He is being completely unselfish. So he is motivated... no, he is compelled now to use all the opportunities and resources he has to tell everyone about Jesus.

Paul shows his passion again when he writes to the church in Corinth. At one point he is defending his apostleship and talks about those in ministry should be taken care of. But then he reveals a little more of his heart and his above-and-beyond willingness to serve:

For when I preach the gospel, I cannot boast, since I am compelled to preach. Woe to me if I do not preach the gospel!

-1 Corinthians 9:16

I get the feeling that if we were to meet Paul, he would be this guy who just radiated passion for Christ. You know what I mean? He would be the kind of guy you get around and soak up so much wisdom and knowledge about how to live for Christ. With that drive he had and no-nonsense attitude, though, most also feel conviction. At the least, most Christians today have no idea how to relate with Paul and his convictions whatsoever. I hear this a lot from various people in church, that the great commission, or the calling of the church to go and make disciples, is only for certain people in the church. Typically that is considered to be leaders in ministry and leaders in the church. But I disagree with that. I believe this calling is for every person who is a follower of Christ. Read this quote from MacLaren's *Expositions*:

> Let us remember, too, that, just because this commission is given to the whole church, it is binding on every individual member of the church. There is a very common fallacy, not confined to this subject, but extending over the whole field of Christian duty, by which things that are obligatory on the community are shuffled off the shoulders of the individual. But we have to remember that the whole church is nothing more than the sum total of all its members, and that nothing is incumbent upon it which is not in their measure incumbent upon each of them. Whatsoever Christ says to all, He

'says to each, and the community has no duties
which you and I have not.[8]

The calling to share this life-saving, life-changing
message is for everyone who starts to follow Jesus. I want to
go back to the words of Paul. As I have been sitting here
writing this and studying, more and more of Paul's heart is
jumping out at me. We have to remember his life and where he
came from. Yeah, Paul was a knowledgeable guy and trained
in the law, but before following Christ he was trying to get as
many Christians killed and thrown in jail as he could. He was
just as passionate about that. You know his past life had to be
weighing on him at this time in his life. "How could I have
held such beliefs? How could I be so cruel?"

And after his supernatural meeting with Jesus, where
his life was dramatically altered for greater, Paul was
overwhelmed by the grace and love of God. And that is what
is swelling up inside him that pushes its way out. "Woe to me
if I do not preach the gospel!"

Paul had the freedom to not speak about Christ if he
wanted to. But hear me on this: if he had chosen to hold that
transforming message to himself, would he really have been a
follower of Christ? I'm not trying to stir up an
Arminian/Calvinist debate. I just think Paul understood what
had taken place in his life. Unconditional love and grace had
touched his life to the point he could genuinely say he was
compelled to preach. Paul was trying to convey here in 1
Corinthians 9 that he would truly be miserable if he did not

mold his whole life to living out the gospel and telling everyone about Jesus.

Let me be completely honest with you. I am not there. I want to be, but I am just being real with you. I am a work in progress and this hits me hard because I know I need to take steps to be the way Paul was.

Paul goes on in this chapter to powerfully articulate how this practically looks in his life. And by the way, every church and Christian needs to adopt this approach to reaching those outside the church:

> Though I am free and belong to no one, I have made myself a slave to everyone, to win as many as possible. To the Jews I became like a Jew, to win the Jews. To those under the law I became like one under the law (though I myself am not under the law), so as to win those under the law. To those not having the law I became like one not having the law (though I am not free from God's law but am under Christ's law), so as to win those not having the law. To the weak I became weak, to win the weak. I have become all things to all people so that by all possible means I might save some. I do all this for the sake of the gospel, that I may share in its blessings.

-1 Corinthians 9:19-23

I don't know where you are in your life. I don't know if this makes you feel terrible about yourself because you realize you don't measure up. That was not my intention here. I am convinced, however, that every single one of us who follow Jesus need to have a life-altering encounter with Him. It is not just something that might be good, or something to consider. This is a necessity.

Why are you holding back this message that you know completely shattered your old world? Can you really say you are compelled to tell the world about Jesus? Here's my answer to you on how to get there. Remember, I'm just a guy on this journey as well. This is what I see: we need to get on our knees, pray to God with a genuine and authentic passion to hear from Him, and be shown what He wants us to do.

Then we have to crack open our Bibles, pull out our highlighters and pens, and get to work in there. The scriptures come alive to us when we are open and receptive to them! But here's the place where I see a lot of us will fall off and never go any further. We saw this in the last chapter. We have to do what it says. We have to tell the world!

How, then, can they call on the one they have not believed in? And how can they believe in the one of whom they have not heard? And how can they hear without someone preaching to them? And how can anyone preach unless they are sent? As it is written: "How beautiful are the feet of those who bring good news!"

-Romans10:14-15

Chapter 12

God Doesn't Need Me to Defend Him

"For some people, God is an old man with a beard sitting on a throne out in space somewhere. If that's the kind of God they don't believe in, then I agree with them."
–Greg Koukl

When I was in graduate school, I remember being introduced to Christian apologetics. I was still a fairly young Christian, so there was a ton of stuff I was still learning. Apologetics, to me, was empowering. In the beginning, I was looking at it wrong. I truly felt I had learned a discipline that gave me the ability to make it impossible for anyone to deny the existence of God. I really believed I could prove the truthfulness of Christianity.

Over time, however, I realized I didn't have the ability I

thought I had with apologetics. If someone doesn't want to believe in God and wants to continue in disbelief, then the person will do what he or she wants. I couldn't force anyone to believe in God. Honestly, that was kind of tough to learn. It wasn't so much a pride thing, thinking I had the ability to do that. It was more defeating and frustrating. I passionately wanted everyone to believe, so I saw apologetics as a great way to achieve that.

Let's talk about Christian apologetics, which in the simplest terms, is giving a rational defense for Christianity. Let me just say here, though, that I'm not going to go really deep into this practice. There are a lot of great works out there that I would recommend. My purpose is to point you in this direction of learning to know what you believe and how to share that.

> But in your hearts revere Christ as Lord. Always
> be prepared to give an answer to everyone who
> asks you to give the reason for the hope that you
> have. But do this with gentleness and respect,

> -1 Peter 3:15

The early church took this seriously. They were ready and willing to defend the truth of God and His word any chance they got. So, up front here, my purpose is simply to ignite that same fire and sense of mission they had in doing this. Using apologetics should be considered a part of the Christian's duty.

One of the most overused phrases in our postmodern culture is "That may be true for you, but it's not true for me." That statement raises my blood pressure (I probably should work on that) whenever I hear it. It is not the end-the-conversation, knock-down-argument point that many believe it to be. It is simply false. I don't understand how we as rational-thinking people can fall for this line.

I don't want to trash you if you have said this and you are just not aware of its implications. Relativism implies there is a truth ("there is no truth" is a truth statement). But what it really means is, "Just don't challenge what I like to think because I don't like that." So really it comes down to not wanting to feel convicted or not wanting to get our feelings hurt.

Ok, so I want to make it known clearly what my intentions are with apologetics and why I see it is absolutely necessary for the church to be on board with it. First off, the early church used apologetics to defend and spread the gospel and they did it effectively. Secondly, apologetics is oftentimes wrongly assumed to be a secondary issue in Christianity. Sometimes people look at apologetics as merely a philosophical, intellectual practice the only real purpose of which is to consume the time of those who like to argue and make their brains hurt. Right? Seriously, I have spoken to many people who completely remove anything Biblical from their perception of apologetics.

Before starting our church, I was discouraged from making apologetics an important part of our ministry. What infuriated me was this advice came from people who were part of a church-planting organization. We're in a world of over seven billion people, with thousands upon thousands of different denominations of Christianity, and many religions. According to every statistic I've seen, Christianity is still the largest religious group in the world, but Islam is threatening to overtake that spot in the near future, and third is the unaffiliated with over one billion people strong.

If you're reading this and you're not a Christian, then this probably doesn't mean as much to you. But I am speaking to pastors and Christians—all people in God's church—we have to be willing to engage people. Do you care if people get this message? Don't you care if people are receiving the real message of hope through Christ? Am I trying to put pressure on you and make you feel convicted? Yep! I'm not even going to hide.

Maybe this will help you if you have had an issue with apologetics, or have just been exposed to someone who had improper motivations in using it. I'll argue that doing our Christian duty of apologetics stems from love. How so? Well, Jesus was once asked what the greatest commandment was. And He said, "Love the Lord your God with all your heart and with all your mind and with all your soul." Then He went on to say that the second was just like it: "Love your neighbor as yourself." He didn't leave anything out or change the law in any way. He perfectly and succinctly rehashed it.

So basically, He said numbers one through four are about your vertical relationship with God and numbers five through ten have to do with your horizontal relationship with people. If you say something wrong and hurtful about my wife or daughter, then we are going to have some problems. I will stand up for them. My horizontal love for them draws me to do it. In the same way, if you are going to claim to be speaking the truth about God and state something wrong and untruthful about Him, then my vertical love for Him compels me to speak up.

"Whoever acknowledges me before others, I will also acknowledge before my Father in heaven. But whoever disowns me before others, I will disown before my Father in heaven.

-Matthew 10:32-33

God is not in desperate need of you and me standing up for Him as if He is being bullied. He doesn't need anything from us. He can snap His finger, twitch His nose, or just think about it and we are wiped out of existence. So let's just understand our places. Apologetics is not the last line of defense for God. Apologetics, rather, is part of the job and calling of believers to share their faith. The more the Christian grows in his or her relationship with God (the vertical love), the more the Christian learns and feels compelled by love to reach out to others (horizontal love).

I want to make this simple. There are just three things the Christian should know when dealing with apologetics. Know what you believe, know why you believe it, and know how to effectively communicate that. That's it! Those of you who are scared off by this, you'll notice I didn't throw in a bunch of philosophical terms that only a Ph.D. grad could comprehend. It is basic stuff that should be part of your repertoire.

Know what you believe

That seems simple enough. I don't think that's asking too much. You should know what you believe. Essentially it is what Jesus was saying when he asked His guys, "Who do you say I am?" Jesus was clearly saying we have to make a decision about Him. Whoever you are reading this, a believer or not, you still have to do something with the person of Jesus. Now you can claim He was not real, or that He was just a man, or even that He was just a really good liar, but you are still forced to make a decision about Him.

So, followers of Christ, you should know what you believe. That seems as if it should go without saying. In all honesty, how can anyone really believe in the gospel if the person doesn't even know it? So I would argue that you have to understand the dire situation you are in.

for all have sinned and fall short of the glory of
God

-Romans 3:23

To see that you need anything, first you have to
understand that you are broken and without hope. I'll just
continue on here with what is commonly called the Romans
Road. If you've grown up in church, or taken any kind of
Bible class, then you've heard this term. It's just a name used
to describe some passages from the letter to the Romans that
speak of salvation.

For the wages of sin is death, but the gift of God
is eternal life in Christ Jesus our Lord.

-Romans 6:23

So we come to an understanding that we are not ok if
we are left to ourselves and that we need help. Then we learn
the only One who can help us is Jesus:

If you declare with your mouth, "Jesus is Lord,"
and believe in your heart that God raised him
from the dead, you will be saved. For it is with
your heart that you believe and are justified, and

it is with your mouth that you profess your faith and are saved.

-Romans 10:9-10

Then Paul comes to chapter ten and gives us the clearest way to show us how we respond to God in faith. It is about our belief and total faith in Jesus, who He is, and what He has done.

"Everyone who calls on the name of the Lord will be saved."

-Romans 10:13

This is what we must understand at the very beginning to be saved. This is what we have to understand about what we believe.

Know why you believe

The next stage is to understand why you believe what you believe. The passage we read earlier from 1 Peter 3:15 told us to be prepared always to share with people why we have hope. So Jesus is basically saying, "I want you to now take this message that has given you hope and share that with the world."

"People are going to ask you questions and be drawn to you because their curiosity will be piqued. You have to be ready to talk." That's what He is saying to His followers. You see, Christians—churches—it is essential that we study and learn what it is we believe so we can be effective witnesses. This is where we see apologetics coming into play.

We are not called to keep this life-giving message to ourselves. To keep this message a secret would have to be the single most selfish action imaginable. We need to understand the gospel so we can share it.

Know how to effectively communicate it

So if you're still following me, just learn the first step really well so you can get to this point. I say "learn to share this effectively" because it is vital. When I say "effectively," I don't necessarily mean you have to be this world-famous orator who can sell broccoli on a stick to a kid at a candy store. It's not about having an amazing ability that you are born with. The last part of 1 Peter 3:15 says, "But do this with gentleness and respect." You might be out there feeling as if you aren't good enough and that you are lacking in qualifications to be an ambassador for God. Welcome to the club because I'm right there with you.

My encouragement to you is to keep the conversation about Jesus. We spoke about how Paul modeled that whenever he talked to people. You don't have to be all fancy. Just lead the conversation to the gospel. We already established that you should know what you believe and why. Is that not enough to share with people? Just look for those opportunities. They will come.

Read Acts 17 where Paul happened to come into the city of Athens and he saw an opportunity. He talked to the people. He didn't back down. You know what he also did? He used their idols as a jumping-off place and even quoted from their own poets to make his point. And then he simply shared the story of Jesus, what He did, who He is, and what He could do for them if they believed.

There is no need to complicate this. Work on witnessing and learn and grow in your understanding. This will only help your effectiveness. Push yourself to take as many opportunities as possible. Your comfort level will only increase and you'll see God open more and more chances for you to tell people about Him.

But don't overcomplicate this. I am convinced that if Christians would come closer to God and get in His presence more every day, then their love for Him would grow exponentially. As a result of being in God's presence and having His love conquer you, you will involuntarily, almost out of reflex, share His message of hope with a passion that can only be described as coming straight from the heart of God.

Chapter 13
I Put This at the End for a Reason

"The blood of the martyrs is the seed of the church."
-Tertullian

I've always been extremely picky when it comes to eating. I was one of those kids that you hated to have over when you were eating because I was used to certain foods and stuck to them. My mom was a really great cook, so I had the best. It was tough going out to eat, particularly at fast-food burger places. First-world problems, I know. Whenever I went anywhere, though, I would ask for a plain burger. I thought it was easy enough. It seemed as if 90% of the time they got it wrong and assumed when I said "plain" that I meant "half" the works. There were times when the burger came out and before I even looked at it, I sent it back.

I'm just kidding! So with my "condition," Subway is a good way to make sure I know what I'm getting on my sandwich. As I've grown older, I have become less and less picky and open to more foods. Socially this is more beneficial to me because it's not as cute for a forty-year-old man to look sad and ask if he can instead have some chicken tenders.

Speaking of first world problems, that is our country now. We have so many options. If you want something to eat, it's ok if you're picky because the choices are seemingly endless. If you can't find what you want in one place, there are always buffets. That doesn't just go for food either. Whatever product you are looking for, there is an option, or just a plethora of choices. That is the American way.

That mentality has reared its ugly head in the church. We want options! We want various styles! We want buffet churches where we can pick and choose the flavor of Jesus worship that makes us feel good. Ok, so that's my rant. I bring that up because in this option-style Christianity we have created, people have naturally styled their walks in Christ with all the desirable and easier teachings of scripture.

What I mean is they leave out things that are either controversial or uncomfortable to follow. One of the things I consistently see in the New Testament church that rarely gets addressed in today's popular Christianity is suffering for being a follower of Christ. There's no shortage of passages that tell us plainly that if we follow Christ, we will suffer, or have struggles and hard times.

Dear friends, do not be surprised at the fiery ordeal that has come on you to test you, as though something strange were happening to you. But rejoice inasmuch as you participate in the sufferings of Christ, so that you may be overjoyed when his glory is revealed.

-1 Peter 4:12-13

Jesus even had difficult and informative conversations with His guys. He didn't hold back. He didn't sugar-coat anything. And He didn't lie to them and try to act as if everything was going to go smoothly for them if they followed Him.

You will be hated by everyone because of me, but the one who stands firm to the end will be saved.

-Matthew 10:22

Every time I am speaking to a new believer, or someone who is asking about what it means to follow Christ, I make it a point to explain that Jesus is asking for more than just you repeating some words after your pastor. My testimony has immensely shaped the way I do ministry. When I was much younger, my family would go to church more regularly. I'm talking when I was a baby. But we stopped going for quite a

few years. I started going back to church with friends and
some other family members when I was eleven. Here's where
my journey, so to speak, began.

I was an extremely shy kid. So there was this one time
when the church was having an invitation time (do you
remember those?) and I felt overwhelmingly drawn to go
forward and talk to the pastor. Now here's the part where I
have learned not to adopt: he had me repeat a certain prayer
after him. I don't blame him, it's just that I had no idea what I
was doing and there was no teaching me or explaining to me
what it meant or what I was supposed to do. So as a result,
nothing happened in my life. I wasn't changed. I never came
to know Christ or receive salvation.

So I went on to live with no real concern for following
Jesus. I really should've been arrested, or at least gotten in
trouble more than I did. I lived a life of doing what I wanted
and partying. Then I remember being seventeen and coming to
the conclusion that I needed to talk to my pastor because I
knew I wasn't saved. I was scared and recognized I needed to
get right with God. The same thing happened, though. "All
right, just kneel down and repeat after me." I repeated his
prayer and then he asked me how I felt. I remember this
moment vividly. I felt as if there was no hope for me. I had
done the last thing I could. I believed I was going to hell. It
wasn't a great feeling to say the least. I lied to him, though, so
he didn't worry.

I ended up graduating later and going to a Christian
college to get some basics out of the way and play some

baseball. They typically had us do dorm devotionals during the week (usually I skipped them). One particular time I went to one and some of the guys were having some moments and confessing some things. I don't really remember everything there. But I do remember I was feeling God strongly calling out to me. I was scared and confused, though. But then I broke down, which I never do.

Now, here's where my story went in a completely different direction. My cousin took me to another room, opened the Bible, and showed me what it meant to follow Christ and what I was doing and needed to do. It had a profound impact on me. I gave my life to Christ in that dorm room when I was nineteen.

I didn't just give you my testimony to take up some time and make this chapter about me. That molded the way I do ministry and I want people to understand what it is they are getting into when they follow Christ (or what they are rejecting in Him). Jesus had some more revealing, yet controversial words. I'm convinced a lot of people reject Him for words such as these:

> Large crowds were traveling with Jesus, and turning to them he said: "If anyone comes to me and does not hate father and mother, wife and children, brothers and sisters—yes, even their own life—such a person cannot be my disciple.

And whoever does not carry their cross and
follow me cannot be my disciple.

-Luke 14:25-27

So I don't know if you caught it, but Jesus' approach
was that when a lot of people showed up to hear from Him, He
dropped the hammer and told it how it was! Jesus didn't take
our culture's approach and give the more palatable message.
He boldly and without hesitation laid out the truth.

Now I bring that up because it's related to the topic of
suffering. Don't ever make the mistake of saying the Bible
never told you that when you started following Jesus that your
life would be difficult, or that the spiritual battle would come
on strong. It absolutely does!

One of my favorite letters in the New Testament is the
one Paul wrote to the Philippians. If you don't know much
about the letter and the context of it, you should. Ok, think
about this: Paul writes this encouraging letter to the
Philippians...from prison! I cannot rave enough about the
unwillingness to quit and all-out focus for the cause of Christ
that Paul exhibited. He perfectly exemplifies what he wrote to
the church in Galatia about not giving up.

Let us not become weary in doing good, for at
the proper time we will reap a harvest if we do

not give up.

-Galatians 6:9

Just writing those words motivates me. Don't we need to hear that so often? I know I do. Don't we need to constantly go back to those words to remind ourselves of that great truth? No doubt! Those words are not just to get us a little pumped up from time to time. They also help us when we come to places like Paul was in. Granted, we may not have experiences as extreme as Paul's in prison, but we still have trials.

Now we've established that Paul is in prison when he writes this letter to the Philippians. It's worth mentioning here too that Paul seems to have a completely radical view compared to most people. He is so sold-out to the mission of Christ that he can look past the unthinkable present situation to a positive that comes out of this. People in the palace were hearing the truth and believers outside were deeply encouraged and now had confidence to share their faith. This was all birthed out of Paul having this focused, glass-half-full type of faith.

I want you to understand where Paul's whole mentality is when he is in prison. He can't be shaken. It seems impossible to take him off the mission. He is so laser focused that whatever happens, he sees the positive.

For to me, to live is Christ and to die is gain.

-Philippians 1:21

Paul knows the cost of following Jesus. He has a firm grip on what it actually means to follow Christ and the consequences that may and most likely will come with that decision. Paul was so devoted to Christ that he was committed to Him whether he stayed on this earth, or whether his life was taken from him. He knew either way he would still always have that connection and relationship.

But whatever were gains to me I now consider loss for the sake of Christ. What is more, I consider everything a loss because of the surpassing worth of knowing Christ Jesus my Lord, for whose sake I have lost all things. I consider them garbage, that I may gain Christ and be found in him, not having a righteousness of my own that comes from the law, but that which is through faith in Christ — the righteousness that comes from God on the basis of faith. I want to know Christ — yes, to know the power of his resurrection and participation in his sufferings, becoming like him in his death, and so, somehow, attaining to the resurrection from the dead.

-Philippians 3:7-11

These are the real, fanatical, but beautiful words of a man who was right in the middle of persecution and suffering. I encourage you to just sit there and meditate on what he is saying there and examine your life in Christ (if you are a follower) and see if you could say those same words with truthfulness.

So back to the suffering part and what Paul says here. Notice how he is saying this, "I want to know Christ, the power of his resurrection and participate in his sufferings." I know I'm making it a point to highlight this unpopular idea of all Christians suffering. This isn't a ploy to elevate an unhealthy ascetic lifestyle. The Bible never endorses any notion that we as followers of Christ should willingly inflict pain on ourselves for the purpose of becoming more holy. So there is no need for you to make your next DIY project a bed of nails for you to lay on with the idea that you are making yourself better. That will do nothing for you, except make your back look like a dart board. Jesus never meant for us to inflict unnecessary pain on ourselves to be more holy. In fact, that would fall under a legalistic, false Christianity instead of the true grace through faith.

Ok, so if this is not a self-infliction type of suffering, then what does the Bible mean? Instead of the Bible telling us,

"Here's what you need to do and suffer to be righteous," it's really telling us, "If you follow Christ, this is what will happen." As I mentioned earlier, Jesus is merely being transparent with us and allowing us to decide if the cost of following Him is worth the new life we will receive. Jesus did big-time things—miracles. He was the fad and the new "new." But He saw through the people's bull and told them the way things really were. "If you want to follow me, you have to be willing to give up everything." Isn't that what Jesus was saying in the Luke 14 passage? He explains it even further, telling us to count the cost:

> "Suppose one of you wants to build a tower. Won't you first sit down and estimate the cost to see if you have enough money to complete it? For if you lay the foundation and are not able to finish it, everyone who sees it will ridicule you, saying, 'This person began to build and wasn't able to finish.'

> "Or suppose a king is about to go to war against another king. Won't he first sit down and consider whether he is able with ten thousand men to oppose the one coming against him with twenty thousand? If he is not able, he will send a delegation while the other is still a long way off and will ask for terms of peace. In the same

way, those of you who do not give up
everything you have cannot be my disciples."

-Luke 14:28-33

The really hard, gut-checking reality is we have to
decide if we are all in with Jesus even if suffering, rejection, or
persecution comes. What Jesus points out, that happens all the
time, is people are good with Jesus at the beginning, but when
one uncomfortable thing comes their way, they are quick to
drop Him and run the other way.

This is why I have a hatred for shallow Christian
teaching. Pastors, when you leave out the controversial stuff
and the things you feel will shrink your crowd, you are not
doing the people any good. You can't save them anyway. God
is the one doing the saving. And He uses His word to convict,
and to grow, and to draw people to Him and the truth. When
you leave out essential truths, how can that be justified to be
good?

Suffering, then, will come if you choose to follow Jesus
by denying yourself, taking up your cross, and following Him.
It just naturally comes. It is not something you put into action.
You may get that by now, but how could Paul speak about
glorying in his sufferings? Look at what he says:

Not only so, but we also glory in our sufferings,
because we know that suffering produces
perseverance; perseverance, character; and

149

character, hope. And hope does not put us to shame, because God's love has been poured out into our hearts through the Holy Spirit, who has been given to us.

-Romans 5:3-5

So don't miss this: there is a purpose behind our suffering in Christ. It is not some sick joke of God's where He is entertained by our struggles. It produces perseverance, which produces character, which produces hope. Read the book of James. He would agree with this and tell us the same.

If you get anything from this chapter, I want you to get this: if you so choose to truly be an authentic follower of Christ and not a pretender, it is a struggle. I don't know what kinds of trials and temptations you'll deal with, or how you'll be abandoned or rejected. But trials will come in some way. That is infinitely small, however, compared to grace, love, and acceptance that God offers you. Dietrich Bonhoeffer states it powerfully in talking about costly grace. "Such grace is costly because it calls us to follow, and it is grace because it calls us to follow Jesus Christ. It is costly because it costs a man his life, and it is grace because it gives a man the only true life."[9]

Is the cost too high for you? Is life in Christ worth giving up everything for? That is what Jesus is asking of you.

Chapter 14
Comfort Zones Are For Wimps!

"A comfort zone is a beautiful place, but nothing
ever grows there."

-Unknown

I have to be honest: writing this book has been
enormously helpful for me. I realize that might sound
extremely vain. "Great, Kyle. So you're saying the book you
wrote is really helpful to *you*?" So I guess if no one gets
anything out of this book, it will at least have been good
therapy for me. Ha!

What I mean is the intense study I had to put into my
efforts here definitely forced me past my comfort points. I am
learning more and more that pushing past the boundaries are
essential to living a fully devoted life to Christ. We've already

looked at James 1, which confirms that comfort zones are the cemeteries where dead faiths go to rest. I actually look forward to challenging myself and stepping out in faith, even when in the past I might have not even considered doing something. I read Paul's words in Philippians 3 with a fresh sense of understanding and excitement:

> Not that I have already obtained all this, or have already arrived at my goal, but I press on to take hold of that for which Christ Jesus took hold of me. Brothers and sisters, I do not consider myself yet to have taken hold of it. But one thing I do: Forgetting what is behind and straining toward what is ahead, I press on toward the goal to win the prize for which God has called me heavenward in Christ Jesus.
>
> -Philippians 3:12-14

I'm telling you, I read those words now and physically it does something to me. Not a repulsion, or sense of confusion, or even fear of having to think that way if I am to be a good Christian. I now read those words and I get it. Listen, I am not perfect. I do not have it all down. I told you in the beginning that these are the words from a guy who is simply a work in progress. But the best way I can describe to you what the God of all creation is doing to this imperfect man is: He is shedding the things of this world from my life and giving me a supernatural clarity for Him and only Him. I've found myself getting excited just to write these words down and share them with you.

So those are my introductory words to my wrapping-it-up chapter. Is that a thing? I used to almost cringe when I would hear people say they were "on a journey with God." I was probably a little self-righteous and holier-than-thou in my thinking. It just didn't seem deep enough to me. It seemed fake.

At this point, though, I am completely comfortable in referring to my walk with God as a journey. It is the perfect depiction of the way I see pursuing Jesus. You have to make a decision to do it. You are stepping out into an area, or a world that is largely, or maybe even completely, unknown to you. There is a perfect balance of excitement and discomfort.

And with that step comes two competing sides. On one side are people telling you, "You're crazy! That is not who you are. There is no way God wants you to do that." On the other side you hear, "Yeah that's awesome! I'm excited for you. That is wild and weird, but if is God talking, then you gotta do it." And one of the difficult parts of this journey is deciphering who to listen to. Maybe the answer to that is to stop taking so much stock in what others say and pick up God's word and do what it says.

That is all I have done with this book and in this whole study. I don't know if you noticed, but I have very few quotes in this book. That was intentional. I'm not preaching for everyone to go isolate themselves from the outside world and never listen to another person. There are countless people all around each of us with an abundance of wisdom. We would do well to learn from them. My purpose in this, however, was simply to go straight to scripture and the leaders in the early church, tune everything else out, and soak in what they absorbed from Jesus.

So my hope is not to cause many of you to look at your church with the stink eye and question everything your leaders do. I don't want to cause some unnecessary revolution that will only create division and unrest. But it is crucial that we stop and examine what it is we are truly doing in church and in Christianity.

Pastors and leaders in ministry: are you in this because you want money, fame, or just to prove to someone who didn't believe in you that you can do it? If you answer "yes" to any of those, you need to take a major step back, repent, and either do something else, or scrap your old plan and start following God's.

Believers who are in the church, out of the church, or maybe somewhere in between: what does it mean for you to actually follow Jesus? What feeling do you get when you read Jesus' words in Matthew?

Whoever does not take up their cross and follow
me is not worthy of me. Whoever finds their life

will lose it, and whoever loses their life for my
sake will find it.

-Matthew 10:38-39

One of the problems we have in a society like I live in
here in the United States is the majority of the people have an
overabundance of stuff. We don't know what it's like to have
to genuinely struggle for anything, let alone the basic
necessities of life.

And with that as the background to our lives, we come
to the gospel and Jesus and our response is, "Ok, so what can
Jesus actually bring to my life that I don't already have?" So
Jesus' words, which are extreme and fanatical, run through our
biased filters and we merely interpret them as being an
exaggeration. I don't think that anymore. Jesus meant what
He said.

Because of this journey I am now on, I ask myself and
God a few questions periodically.   "Am I doing what you
want, God, not what I want?" This question stems from some
powerful, yet challenging texts in Proverbs:

"Two things I ask of you, Lord;
do not refuse me before I die:
Keep falsehood and lies far from me;
give me neither poverty nor riches,
but give me only my daily bread.

155

Otherwise, I may have too much and disown
you and say, 'Who is the Lord?'
Or I may become poor and steal,
 and so dishonor the name of my God.

-Proverbs 30:7-9

Full disclosure here: I don't always like these words or pray them with the truthfulness I should. Can a prayer even be real if you pray it as if you're hoping God's on vacation? Honestly, I don't pray them all the time.

Then, one of the other questions I ask God frequently is, "God am I where you want me to be, doing what you want me to be doing?" It's simple, but they are real questions as I am truly looking for answers from God. And here's the really wild thing—God will respond!

My big prayer and hope in writing this book is that you will take your walk with God seriously. I took an authentic approach to looking at the Bible and attempting to draw out what followers of Christ should do based on what they did in the first church and what God's word says. What else can we do but that?

Church, Christians, get out of the way if you don't want to be all in with God. The other day, my daughter pointed out that I didn't use my blinker when we were in the neighborhood by our house. So I pointed out to her that no one was around. But then I realized I was setting a terrible example. She's going to be driving in a few years (that alone frightened me) and I want her to take driving (every aspect of it) seriously. I want her to drive the right way, even when no one is around.

Let me clarify this a little, though. Christians, don't just do the right things because people are watching you and you don't want to look like a hypocrite. Do the right things because you have been forgiven of your sins and there is no way in this world, or any world, that you deserved that. Don't just do the right things because you want to avoid hell. Do the right things because the God of everything reached out to you in love. And don't just do the right things because your friend, pastor, or church told you to. Do the right things because in Christ you are a new creation.

> Therefore, if anyone is in Christ, the new creation has come: The old has gone, the new is here!
>
> -2 Corinthians 5:17

Those of you who have faith in Jesus, you are new creations. How amazing is that? You may not always feel like it. Your situation might be the same as it was before your faith began. But make no mistake about it, something colossal has happened to you! Something that was not manufactured in your own minds or abilities took place in you. When you placed your faith in Jesus, God took a wretched, undeserving person, welcomed you into His family, and called you His own. I don't know if you're catching my tone, but this is a huge cause for celebration!

So in light of this incredibly amazing news, how then can we authentically pursue Jesus? We realize God isn't asking for some superhuman people to step up. He does the work. He just asks for you to be willing. He is asking you to step up and be willing to live bold, committed, faithful lives to Him—like the kind of lives that are laid out so clearly in the Bible, the kind of lives where the members of the church are actually relating with one another in a closely knit fashion.

When someone needs something, are we there for each other, as we read in Acts 2? When someone is going through something, good or bad, are we in it with them as we read in 1 Corinthians 12? Are we willing to take this life-giving message of hope and salvation to everyone we possibly can, even if we may experience rejection, suffering, or even death?

What does it mean to be an authentic follower of Christ? As I've said repeatedly, I'm still figuring this out as I go. God's still revealing it to me. But as of now, I define it as someone who puts his or her faith in Jesus and never looks back. That person takes God's words seriously and starts to put them into practice in his or her life.

It's not always pretty. You're gonna stumble multiple times along the way. You'll get a ton of scars, but that's ok, because they'll remind you of how far you've come. And then the God of all creation will do a transforming work in your life that no amount of money, fame, or person could even begin to touch. He'll strip away the fake and show you what He always intended for you and your life.

As a result, you'll be left with Him and His truth and love. This, plus experience (although I feel I'm only just beginning the journey), is true joy, overwhelming peace, and indescribable excitement. This is true, genuine life with God.

So I leave you with this question: are you pursuing Jesus with an authentic faith?

Notes

1. The Merriam Webster Dictionary. (1997). (Springfield, MA: Merriam-Webster Incorporated), 221.

2. Elliot, Elisabeth. (2015). "Through Gates of Splendor," p.175, AZ Quotes, Tyndale House Publishers, Inc. https://www.azquotes.com/quote/812844.

3. Taylor, J. Hudson, quoted in Good Reads, Good Read Inc., 2018, https://www.goodreads.com/quotes/799214-the-great-commission-is-not-an-option-to-be-considered.

4. Rouis, Rex. "Faith Is 'hupostasis' – Hebrews 11:1." Hope Faith Prayer, https://www.hopefaithprayer.com/faith/faith-hebrews-hupostasis/.

5. Ross, Hugh. Why The Universe Is The Way It Is. (Grand Rapids: Baker Books, 2008), 38.

6. Grenz, Stanley J., Guretzki, David, and Nordling, Cherith Fee. Pocket Dictionary of Theological Terms. (Downers Grove: Inter Varsity Press, 1999), 85.

7. Jillette, Penn, quoted by Napp Nazworth. Famous Atheist Magician Penn Jillette Cites Bible as a Favorite Book. Christian Post, November 18, 2012, https://www.christianpost.com/news/famous-atheist-

magician-penn-jillette-cites-bible-as-a-favorite-book-85175/.

8. MacLaren's Expositions. Bible Hub. https://biblehub.com/commentaries/1_corinthians/9-16.htm.

9. Bonhoeffer, Dietrich. The Cost of Discipleship. (New York: Simon and Schuster, 1959), 45.